CW00493313

Unbelievable Crimes Volume Two

Unbelievable Crimes, Volume 2

Daniela Airlie

Published by Daniela Airlie, 2023.

While every precaution has been taken in the preparation of this book, the publisher assumes no responsibility for errors or omissions, or for damages resulting from the use of the information contained herein.

UNBELIEVABLE CRIMES VOLUME TWO

First edition. April 12, 2023.

Written by Daniela Airlie.

Table of Contents

Unbelievable Crimes Volume Two...1

Prologue...3

A Monster Disguised As A Human...5

A Mother's Love Knows No Bounds.......................................15

One Truly Twisted Teen...23

A Preventable Murder..31

The Sadistic Student...39

The Lonely Hearts Killers...45

36 Hours Of Hell...57

Three's A Crowd..65

Murdered By Her "Best Friends"...73

Callous Killing Cousins..81

Lord Of The Dolls..91

Final Thoughts..99

I have asserted the right of Daniela Airlie as the publisher and owner of this work in accordance with the Copyright, Designs and Patents Act 1988. No part of this publication may be reproduced whatsoever in any format without the prior written consent of the publisher. This book is for entertainment and informational purposes only.

Although research from various sources has gone into this book, neither the author nor the publisher will be held responsible for any inaccuracies. To the best of the knowledge of the author, all information within this publication is factually correct, derived from researching these cases thoroughly. The author may offer speculation and/or their opinion throughout this book about the cases covered.

danielaairlie.carrd.co[1]

Prologue

True crime has captivated our attention for centuries, and it's not difficult to understand why. The human mind is a complex and fascinating thing, and when it's capable of committing unspeakable acts, it becomes even more intriguing. The history of true crime goes way back to ancient times, when accounts of murders and violent crimes were recorded by way of paintings, sculptures, and even hieroglyphics depicting macabre scenes. While true crime as we know it today is covered in a very different way, the core concept of why we consume it is still there: we're intrigued as to how our fellow men and women can be capable of such atrocities.

However, as humans have evolved over the years, so have our levels of empathy and compassion. These days, true crime followers know that behind every true crime story, there are real victims. In our modern world, it's less about sensationalizing the killers and more about understanding that the victims deserve to have their voices heard. My intent for this series is to cover lesser-known crimes, in turn ensuring that the suffering that the victims endured isn't forgotten. We will remember the monsters that carried out these crimes for the brutality they inflicted on another human being and the unimaginable pain and suffering they forced upon their victims.

If you've followed true crime for years, like me, then you might think you've heard just about every single case out there. Often, true crime documentaries and TV shows only cover the "big headline" criminals, and we get to know these cases inside out. Think of serial killers like Bundy or Ramirez - both heavily covered on TV and in books, and they've often been glorified for their vile acts - and I bet you know at least *some* things about their cases. But what if I told you the name

Shana Grice? Or Mary Vincent? Or Thadius Phillips? These people are victims of some truly deplorable crimes from truly deplorable criminals, and I'll cover their stories in these pages.

With that in mind, as always, I'd like to offer a quick word of caution about some of the cases I'll cover in this book. Some of these crimes are particularly brutal to hear about, including ones involving sexual assault, torture or crimes involving children. This book touches on cases that involve these themes. With that said, let's begin.

A Monster Disguised As A Human

Los Angeles in the 70s was the place to be if you were a teenager. At least, that's what most adolescents thought while dreaming of leaving their boring small towns to chase the sun, sea, and possibly stardom. The free-loving, carefree vibes of the 60s had turned California into a hippy utopia, a movement spilling over into the 70s to make LA seem like the place where dreams were made.

For young Mary Vincent, moving to California seemed like the best way to escape her drab life in Las Vegas, where she was forced to endure the messy fallout of her parents' divorce. Aged just 15, Mary made her way to LA, hitchhiking at a time when it was deemed safe. As we now know, hitchhiking is indeed unsafe when you tally up all of the horrific murders, rapes, and assaults that have ever occurred as a result of a trusting "thumber" hopping into the vehicle of a madman. However, this was 1978, and hitchhiking was merely seen as a vagrant's way of getting about and not an uncommon sight at all.

In her bid to get to California, Mary even slept rough and sometimes broke into vehicles to get a better night's rest. She had an end goal to reach a family member's house, which she eventually got to. However, Mary soon realized that life in LA wasn't everything she'd been dreaming of. No cool hippy commune invited her to join, she had no friends to hang out with, and living with older relatives didn't feel like the most impressive way to rebel. So, with the mirage of LA well and truly faded, Mary headed back to Vegas. Just like before, she would hitchhike her way home, but this time, she would stumble upon the worst kind of evil. The man she would cross paths with carried out acts so vulgar you'd think they only occur in horror movies.

Sadly, 50-year-old Lawrence Singleton would prove that depraved acts of violence and torture aren't merely reserved for the big screen. There are truly sick individuals out there, and Singleton ranks among the sickest.

On September 29, 1978, Mary set about hitchhiking, where she met a young couple who were also looking for a ride. After a short stint thumbing in the midday heat, the trio eventually struck lucky when a van pulled over to the group. It was an older man, someone who Mary would describe as looking like a "grandfather" behind the wheel. His vehicle was empty, with enough room for the three of them to sit in comfortably. However, the man said only one person could hitch a ride, and he picked Mary out as his chosen passenger. The two other hitchhikers warned Mary that the man seemed shady and advised her not to take the offer of a lift.

However, Mary had been sleeping rough and didn't know where her next meal was going to come from. She was tired, hungry, and homesick. She just wanted to get back to the comfort of her parents; even though they were arguing and the atmosphere was full of animosity, it was still home. She deliberated for a split second before her desire to get back home overrode her uncertainty about getting in the van. She hopped in and said goodbye to her fellow hitchhikers, who felt uneasy about letting the young girl drive off with the strange man.

Any uneasiness Mary felt soon evaporated when Lawrence Singleton headed in the direction of her destination. He seemed friendly enough, and the chatter was similar to how a grandparent would speak to you. Singleton looked much older than his 50 years, with more hair on his wiry eyebrows than on his heavily receded hairline. His face was weathered, heavily pockmarked, and lined. He seemed harmless, so when Mary found her eyes getting heavy, she allowed herself to drift off and catch up on some much-needed sleep.

When she awoke, however, she could see Singleton was driving in the wrong direction. Mary's feeling of safety was suddenly swapped for distrust, and she told the older man to turn his van around, and that he knew fine well he was heading the wrong way. Singleton continued to head in the wrong direction until some stern words from the feisty teenager caused him to turn around. "It was an honest mistake," the man told his young passenger, "I just missed the turn off." Content with his answer and relieved that he was now heading in the right direction, Mary felt somewhat at ease again.

After a short while, Singleton said he needed to pull over to pee. Mary used the pit stop to stretch her legs and took a quick walk around the van to get the blood flowing in her legs again. When she looked down at her feet, she could see the laces in her sneakers were loose. She stretched down to tie them up, and as she did, Singleton crept up behind her and struck her head with a blunt object. As the teen fell to the floor, her attacker began punching her. He then grabbed her head and forced the dazed teen to perform a sex act on him.

Eventually, Singleton dragged Mary up off the floor and threw her into the back of his van. He threatened her life if she dared scream, a command the girl heeded. Depraved Singleton tied Mary's hands behind her back and raped her repeatedly. When he was done, he jumped from the back of his van and got into the front, still naked, and drove a little more. Again, he pulled over in a desolate area and resumed his sickening attack. He had a jug of alcohol that he forced the teen to drink in between attacks, and eventually, Mary passed out.

When she awoke, she was forced to lie down on the side of the road. Begging to be set free, the teen tried to plead with her attacker's human side. It turns out he didn't have one. "You want to be free?" the cruel man goaded his vulnerable victim. "I'll set you free." He then grabbed a hatchet from his van and straddled Mary before raining a heavy blow onto her forearm, just below the elbow. With one arm, he rained blows, with the other, he held his victim down. After three whacks of the sharp hatchet, Singleton stood up and observed what he'd just done. Mary could see her arm was still clinging onto her attacker, but she was still lying on the ground. She'd held onto Singleton so tightly that when he chopped her arm off, it clung onto him. He flailed around, trying to remove the limb from himself before setting about chopping Mary's other arm off.

Again, he rained blows onto the poor girl's extremity before severing it completely.

He stood above his naked victim, whom he'd defiled, mutilated, and was now about to leave for dead. "Okay, now you're free," he said as he threw the girl 30 feet down a steep embankment, leaving her to die from blood loss.

Except Mary didn't die.

She was falling in and out of consciousness, crawling as far as she could out of the canyon before losing consciousness again. You can only imagine the sheer terror and panic she would have felt each time she awoke from passing out, suddenly waking up in a situation from hell. I picture it like waking up from a deep sleep. Often, you have a 10-second period after waking from not remembering your worries, anxieties, or your problems. Then, after those few seconds of bliss, reality hits you like a ton of bricks. For Mary, that reality was so barbaric and torturous it certainly puts your typical day-to-day worries and concerns into perspective.

Cleverly, Mary also did her best to pack her wounded arms with mud to stop the bleeding as much as she could. She also held them high, as much as she could anyway, to further prevent blood loss. After what seemed like an eternity, she made her way out of the steep canyon. Still, the area was desolate and passersby were few and far between. *Perhaps Singleton was still combing the area to make sure she was definitely dead, or perhaps a car passing would contain yet another monster with blood and lust on his mind...* but any fears Mary had were faced when she made a difficult three-mile walk to Interstate 5. The determination she had to survive is commendable to say the least, unlike the first car Mary came across on the highway. When the driver saw the bloodied, naked, arm-less young girl stumbling toward them, they sped away as quickly as they could. The teenager's faith in people had been tested throughout this ordeal, but luckily, the second car who spotted the dying girl pulled over and took her straight to the hospital.

She underwent surgery and was given prosthetic arms. This was the late 70s, however, and prosthetics weren't as sophisticated as they are now. With money not being in abundance for Mary, she customized the prosthetics she was given by taking apart old appliances like fridges and stereos. The end product saw Mary's hands being replaced with makeshift metal hooks, a new normal she would have to get used to. Her dream of dancing at Lido de Paris in Vegas had been cruelly stripped away from her most brutally.

As well as the physical changes she was forced to deal with, the psychological trauma was also something Mary had to face. Not only was she left with life-changing injuries, but she'd been through something so barbaric and traumatic that there was no way she'd have any chance of some recovery without intense psychotherapy.

With Mary seeing her attacker face to face for hours, she was able to offer police a detailed description of him. A sketch was drawn up that looked incredibly accurate; the furrowed brow, the lined skin, the distinctive nose, and barely there hair of Lawrence Singleton were all described so specifically by Mary that the police drawing was more like a portrait. So detailed was the sketch that Singleton was quickly identified and arrested for the heinous crime.

Of course, the twisted man would deny any involvement in the attack, meaning Mary had to testify against her rapist in court. In fact, he told lie after lie, all with the intent to discredit Mary. She was a sex worker, he told the court, in much cruder language, whom he paid $10 for her services. It was the teenager who attacked *him*, he insisted. And the two hitchhikers who also identified him as the man who picked Mary up? According to Singleton, they were in on it.

After bravely taking the stand against Singleton, Mary stepped down from her seat and made her way out of court, but her attacker would confront her as she walked away. "I'll finish this job if it takes me the rest of my life," Singleton spat at his teenage victim. This filled Mary with fear, worried that should he be found not guilty, he'd come back and torture her until death this time around.

Thankfully, Lawrence Singleton's plethora of lies were dismissed, and he was found guilty of kidnapping and raping Mary, as well as her attempted murder. However, it wasn't that much of a relief for Mary: her attacker was only sentenced to 14 years behind bars, as was the maximum allowed in California at that time. "I would send him to prison for the rest of his natural life," the judge said as he was sentenced, "If I had the power." Even more frustratingly, Singleton served just over half of his sentence and was released after only eight years. The promise to end Mary's life became a real fear for her. Now in her 20s, the young woman had given birth to two boys and was trying to build a normal life for herself. With Singleton free to roam the streets again, she understandably fretted that he'd find out where she lived and slaughter her and her babies.

Singleton was able to secure early release through good behavior and his willingness to help out by teaching other prisoners. What he refused to do throughout his sentence, however, was accept culpability for the violence and brutality carried out on Mary Vincent, nor would he show any repentance. As a result, there was no way for the convict to show any resolve to never carry out such a merciless attack should he be released. The outcry over Singleton's paltry sentence resulted in a new legislation in California being passed called the "Singleton Bill," which blocks the early release of any offender who has committed a crime involving torture.

He was initially sent to Contra Costa County, but the community here refused to accept him. He was driven out of every community and county he was sent to, with angry crowds arriving at his new home, protesting his presence. Wherever the police sent the offender, a baying crowd would follow to ensure Singleton didn't stick around for long. They weren't always peaceful, either, causing Singleton to be given a bullet-proof vest to wear as he was escorted from one location to the next. In the end, it was clear that no community would accept someone as monstrous as the man they dubbed "The Mad Chopper." Eventually, it was decided Singleton would be given a trailer to live in - on San Quentin prison grounds. He resided in his hiding hole for a year before moving to Florida.

Here, he'd quickly get into trouble, this time for petty theft. In 1990, he was again jailed for stealing a disposable camera and a hat. The items totaled $13. When he was sentenced for these crimes, Singleton told the judge he was merely a "muddleheaded old man," although his attempt at using his age to avoid time in jail failed. He was handed two years behind bars.

By the time 1997 rolled around, Singleton had been back on the streets of Tampa for a good few years and had avoided getting in trouble with the law. Until the spring of that year, when police were called to his Sulphur Springs home. A painter working on a property close by caught a glimpse inside Singleton's window and witnessed a most sickening sight: the naked, older man covered in blood, repeatedly stabbing a naked woman on his couch. He lasted ten years from his release in 1987 before striking again on another unsuspecting female. The frustrating part is that there was never a question of if Singleton would strike again; it was always when. His lack of accountability, remorse, and willingness to reform showed us that.

The painter who saw Singleton's vile attack on the woman would tell of the awful noises the repeated stabs made. He said he could hear the blade hitting the victim's bones. Police arrived at the crazed man's house and found the nude killer to be none other than "The Mad Chopper."

Laid in his living room was Roxanne Hayes. She was a sex worker whom Singleton had paid $20 for her services. He stated that Roxanne took more than the agreed amount from him and threatened him with a knife. While restraining her and taking the knife from her, he says the struggle saw her suffer multiple stab wounds. Sinister Singleton would try to lessen his culpability in this heinous crime, but he forgot there was a witness who saw the whole attack unfold: the painter. He would testify that the victim was laid motionless while Singleton rained down blows with the knife. He saw no struggle; after all, a dead person can't defend themselves. Back behind bars, cowardly Singleton tried to take his own life.

The death of Roxanne Hayes wasn't covered by the press quite like the attack on Mary Vincent. Both were vile, but since Roxanne was a sex worker with a lengthy rap sheet, the headlines weren't as empathetic. They never mentioned her by name, just by profession. What they would often omit was that Roxanne was a mother of three, had a long-term partner and sex work was the profession she found herself in after a life of abandonment by those who ought to have protected her. The 31-year-old had endured a lot in her short life, which ended in a most brutal and violent way.

Singleton's trial began in the spring of 1998. Mary, who for years feared this dreaded day would come, flew to Florida to testify against her attacker for Roxanne. Speaking to the court, Mary, now in her 30s, told of the horrors Singleton put her through when she was a teenager. Quiet but articulate, Mary spoke of the rapes she endured, the beatings, and the vile threats thrown her way from Singleton. She explained how he'd cut her arms off using a hatchet.

The defense team working for Singleton knew there was no way to outright deny his guilt in this crime. After all, he was caught quite literally red-handed. But, they denied he was in his right mind when he carried out the attack. Their argument was that he hadn't set out to kill Roxanne Hayes, an argument that was dismissed when Singleton was found guilty of first-degree murder. He was sentenced to death.

He never made it to the chair, however. In December 2001, cancer caught him before justice could.

Despite the unthinkable things Mary Vincent endured, she did her best to live a normal life in the years following her ordeal. As well as becoming a mother, she founded the Mary Vincent Foundation, which helps children and adolescents who have been the victims of sexual assaults.

Not only that, but she found a love for art despite her claim that she could barely draw a straight line before the attack. Now, she's a highly praised artist despite having what many would view as limitations: prosthetic arms. The love Mary found in her artwork has given her purpose, passion, and an outlet.

Still, there's one thing she wished she'd had the chance to do: look Singleton in his eyes as he met his maker in the electric chair. "I wanted to see his eyes. Eyes are important. When he was on top of me, I was looking at the ax, trying to stay alive," she would say of her unfulfilled wish to look her attacker in the eye. While she never got to have this closure, Mary is adamant she's going to live a life full of purpose and accomplishment, things Singleton surely didn't know the meaning of.

A Mother's Love Knows No Bounds

Films and TV shows would have you believe that cold-blooded killers are hooded figures who lurk in the darkness, waiting for the chance to strike on their next unsuspecting victim. The truth is, we are just as likely to be a victim of someone we know as someone we don't. Many murder cases often expose family members or supposed friends of the victim as being guilty of their murder. All too often, it's jilted ex-spouses, jealous lovers, or rage-fueled arguments with friends that turn deadly. In the case I'm about to cover, a young man decided the best way out of his dire financial situation was to murder his parents.

However, this isn't a black-and-white tale of murder for money. There are plenty of twists throughout Christopher Porco's tale, perhaps the most surprising being that his mother Joan would go on to defend him despite the fact he tried to kill her brutally.

Christopher Porco was a student at the University of Rochester, New York, four hours away from his family home in the quaint hamlet of Delmar. The Porco's were comfortable financially and appeared to be a happy, stable family to those on the outside looking in. Joan and Peter did everything they could to make sure their sons, Christopher and his brother Jonathan, would be successful in life. Good grades were important to the Porco parents, and in return for taking college seriously, the Porco's offered their kids financial support when needed.

This didn't stop Christopher from butting heads with his parents. In 2004, he was clashing with his mother and father on a regular basis, often about his grades. Just the year prior, in 2003, Christopher had to leave university due to his poor grades. He told his parents that it was his professor's fault for misplacing his exam and re-enrolled the following year. However, he took out a loan and forged his father's name as a co-signatory. The $30,000 he illegally loaned was to cover tuition and living expenses, including a new truck.

Christopher told his parents that he had been readmitted to Rochester, leading them to think tuition was covered due to their "mistake" with his exam the year prior. However, his deceitful ways would soon be discovered. At the beginning of November 2004, Peter found out he had cosigned the lease of a brand new yellow truck as well as a large loan. This, of course, was news to him. He quickly tried to get hold of his son, who'd been screening his calls for weeks prior to this. Again, Peter was ignored, so he sent his son an email. *What the hell are you doing*, the email read, *I'm calling the bank to tell them I'm not going to be a cosigner*. Again, the concerned father was ignored.

Still, Peter was lenient with his son, and sent him another email, warning that if he abused his credit again, he'd be filing a forgery claim against him. In the same email, he reached out the olive branch to Christopher, expressing that he and Joan still loved their son, regardless. Two weeks would pass before the Porco parents would see Christopher again, although it would be under circumstances they'd not have been able to imagine in a million years. They knew their son had issues being honest, but they never had the slightest clue he'd been harboring a sickeningly violent streak.

By the middle of November 2004, the seemingly perfect family unit would be dismantled by Christopher horrifically violently. In the early hours of the morning on November 15, the disgruntled 21-year-old made his way into the family home while his parents were sleeping. Wielding a firefighter's ax, he cut the phone lines, turned the burglar alarm off, and crept to his parent's bedroom. He rained blows on his mother and father, mutilating their faces as he bludgeoned them with the sharp blade.

He fled the bloody scene, leaving behind the dead bodies of the people who'd brought him into this world. So Christopher thought, at least.

Peter Porco, by some miracle, managed to get himself out of bed despite his savage wounds. Dripping blood from his extensive head injuries, he walked from the marital bedroom and headed downstairs. He didn't call the police, however; he emptied the dishwasher instead. He even wrote a check to pay for one of Christopher's parking tickets before making himself a packed lunch for work. He continued his usual morning routine in the most unusual of circumstances, even going to collect the newspaper from his front garden. Upon retrieving the paper, he finally collapsed as he got back to the house.

As the blood pooled around him, Peter eventually died from his extensive injuries. He'd been struck 16 times in his skull with such force that part of his jaw had been hacked off.

Known for being reliable and punctual, Peter's workplace got worried when he didn't show up that morning without communicating with them. They called up law enforcement, who headed to his home to carry out a welfare check. When the officer entered the Porco property, he immediately called for backup.

Officers quickly arrived at the crime scene, which was a bloodbath. Peter was immediately pronounced dead, but when the police headed upstairs, they discovered a second victim who was still alive - barely. Joan Porco was missing an eye as well as bits of her skull, but she was miraculously still breathing. She was quickly taken to hospital, and on the journey there was able to confirm who the crazed axeman was: her son, Christopher Porco. Soon after naming her attacker, she was put into a coma due to the extent of her injuries. Nobody knew if Joan would make it, but at least the police had the name of the person responsible for this abhorrent attack.

Immediately, police began looking into Christopher as their prime suspect, focusing their labor force and attention solely on him. The suspect denied any wrongdoing, insisting that he'd been in his dorm lounge on the night of the killing, where he fell asleep and awoke to the shocking news of his dad's murder.

Police had collected evidence to suggest otherwise, though.

The Porco's neighbor spotted Christopher's truck outside the family home in the early hours, around the time the attack happened. It was unlikely the eagle-eyed witness was wrong: the truck was a distinctive bright yellow. It wasn't just the Delmar resident who spotted Christopher's vehicle, either. The unusual-colored truck was spotted speeding through toll booths, which was memorable to the staff at the booths. Separate workers recalled the expensive vehicle going from Rochester to Albany, with one toll collector noting that he remembered the high speed the truck was going as it approached him.

He left his Rochester campus around 10:30 pm and returned shortly after 8:00 am the following day on November 15. Already, there were major holes in Christopher's version of events, not to mention the fact that his mother had confirmed to a police officer that it was her youngest son who'd committed the brutal crime. It was clear as day he was lying, and any attempt to claim that he wasn't driving his yellow truck that night was vetoed by his DNA being found on one of his toll tickets. There was no way Christopher had spent the night on campus like he claimed. He was quickly arrested for the murder of his father and attempted murder of his mother.

A shock twist in the case came when Joan Porco awoke from her medically induced coma. When she was being driven to the hospital after the savage attack, police confirmed with Joan that her son was the ax-wielding attacker. She nodded "yes" when asked if the culprit was Christopher Porco and shook her head "no" when asked if it was her eldest son, Jonathan. She had also accurately answered other questions the officer had in this manner. This changed as soon as Joan had come round from the coma. She insisted that her son was innocent and that the actual killer was still out on the loose. She went as far as writing a letter to urge the police to let her innocent son go and seek out the true killer. Christopher Porco was still maintaining his innocence, too.

Joan accompanied her son to his trial for murder and attempted murder, her face disfigured from the attack he was accused of carrying out. Still, the prosecution had a wealth of incriminating evidence against Christopher, as well as some damning information about his character.

It was revealed to the jury about Christopher's multiple lies to obtain loans and cars in his father's name, suggesting he was sociopathic in his actions. He lacked remorse for his deceitful ways and continued to lie, even when his parents tried to be supportive throughout his duplicitous acts. He was exposed as somewhat of a fantasist, telling other university students that his family owned oceanfront homes and had wealth that far exceeded reality. Christopher's brother, Jonathan, described their sibling relationship as "strained," and it seemed like there was no love lost between the pair.

The jury was also told of Christopher's job at a vet. His role included cleaning up blood after surgeries, something that piqued the jurors' interest. Neither Peter nor Joan Porco's blood was anywhere to be found on Christopher or in his truck, which was hard to understand considering the brutality of the murder and the amount of blood both victims lost. It was surmised that perhaps Christopher's training on properly cleaning up large amounts of blood helped him to ensure he was free of any blood spatter or incriminating DNA.

More incriminating facts came to light as the trial went on. As well as numerous episodes of antisocial behavior, it was revealed Christopher had previously stolen from his parents. In the winter of 2002, he staged a break-in at the Porco home and stole two expensive laptops. In the summer of 2003, he stole a laptop from his parents and sold it online. However, he was also known to deceive those he sold the devices to and often wouldn't ship the items once the buyer had already paid for them. In order to get any disgruntled customers off his back, Christopher would email these unhappy patrons and tell them his brother had passed away, using this lie to explain why he'd been unable to deliver their goods.

The defense was dealing with a lot of character assassinating details from the prosecution, but they offered up a bunch of their own evidence that they were sure would get Christopher off the hook. This, coupled with his mother insisting he wasn't the attacker, could be enough to sway the jury. Sure, Christopher wasn't exactly likable or trustworthy going off the way he lived his life, but does that make someone a killer?

The defense made a point of reminding the jury that none of Christopher's fingerprints were found on the ax used in the attack. As well as this, the defense attorney threw the Bethlehem Police Department's credibility into the mix, explaining how they're not used to dealing with such macabre and disturbing cases and, as such, botched up their investigation when they attended the crime scene.

It was also brought to light that Peter Porco had links to the Bonanno crime family in New York. His uncle Frank was a captain in the family's ranks, and although Peter had no direct involvement with the mafia, it was suggested that his murder was in retaliation for some of Frank's shady dealings.

By the beginning of August 2006, the jury was sent away to deliberate Christopher Porco's case. It took them just a few hours to find him guilty of the second-degree murder of his father and guilty of the attempted murder of his mother. He was handed a minimum of 50 years behind bars for his crimes, 25 years for each victim. Judge Jeffrey Berry noted that Christopher's sentence reflects the real fear that he would re-offend in a similar fashion in the future.

Despite being found guilty, Christopher maintained his innocence, echoing his mother's insistence that the actual killer was still walking the streets. In a post-conviction interview, Christopher said that although the true ax-wielding maniac is out there, he holds little hope they'd ever be caught.

In 2022, Christopher appealed his sentence after serving 16 years in jail. Again, his mother stood by him, writing a sworn affidavit in a bid to help her son obtain a new trial. In her letter, she outlines that she still believes Christopher to be unjustly behind bars. She also acknowledges that Christopher had "refused to conduct himself as he was raised to act" but that his dishonesty and antisocial behavior prior to the attack doesn't make him guilty.

She also mentions that there were fingerprints of an unknown person on the phone box outside her property. The phone box was scarcely, if ever, used, she says, and her phone line that was cut was mere inches away from this area, leading her to conclude the person who used the phone also cut her wires. She continues that the physical and emotional trauma she's dealt with has only been exacerbated by the fact the truth hasn't been sought out by authorities. She concludes that she wants a full hearing for Christopher in order for "truth and facts to prevail."

This case is interesting for so many reasons, but the main point of intrigue for me is the lengths some mothers will go to in order to protect their children. Christopher was found guilty of an unbelievably barbaric crime. He was found to be lying about his whereabouts the morning of the murder, and his vehicle had been seen driving from his campus and to the family home. To top that all off, just hours after the attack, Joan named her son as the culprit.

What would cause Joan to suddenly amend her story? Could it be she couldn't bear to face the fact her son would try to kill her, disfiguring her and taking one of her eyes in the process? Maybe she knows deep down her son is the axeman who killed her husband, but if she maintains her son's innocence, then maybe it'll become reality? Or could it be that Joan truly can't remember the ordeal and genuinely doesn't believe her son to be capable of such a devastating attack toward her? The trauma and emotional wounding of such a horrific attack could be a cause for memory loss. Perhaps, as Joan has been saying for almost two decades now, Christopher **is** innocent; although the courts seem adamant that's certainly not the case. It'll be interesting to follow his appeal and see what, if anything, comes of it.

One Truly Twisted Teen

Most boys at age 17 are thinking about hanging out with their friends, daydreaming about their crush, or thinking of ways to get some extra money to do fun stuff at the weekend. Not Joe Clark - he was thinking about inflicting unbearable cruelty on others in horrific ways.

He didn't stop at merely thinking sick thoughts; he sought ways to carry them out. The teen from Baraboo, Wisconsin, exacted the most unthinkable torture on 13-year-old Thadius Phillips for no reason other than he wanted to. The younger boy had done nothing to provoke the older teen; in fact, Thadius had never met his attacker prior to being abducted by him in July 1995. The story of Joe Clark - nicknamed "Bonebreaker" by news outlets when his crimes came to light - tells not only the tale of a deranged young man but also the story of a courageous young boy who fought to stay alive.

Fellow Baraboo native Chris Steiner was a sprightly teenager who rarely acted out. When the 14-year-old disappeared from the family home in July 1994, his parents immediately knew something was amiss. They called the police when Chris was nowhere to be found, and when authorities searched the teens' room, they knew what they were dealing with: an abduction. Chris' bedroom window had been tampered with, and a slice was visible on his window screen. The Steiner's house had muddy footprints leading to their unlocked patio door.

You can imagine the terror and panic the Steiner's felt when police informed them that their little boy had been taken by an unknown assailant. If the parents knew just how evil, brutal, and sadistic their son's abductor was, I can't comprehend the levels of pain and angst they would have felt.

Joe Clark had snatched the young boy and taken him to his home with one intention: to inflict as much physical brutality on the child as possible. Police had no real clues as to where the young teen had been taken, and the case was as cold as could be. Chris' fate was only discovered when another teen fell into Clark's cruel clutches.

Fast forward to one year later, 17-year-old Joe's lust for torture remained, and he yet again sought out another young boy to carry out acts of violence on. Thadius, or Thad to his friends, had been watching television in the living room when he drifted off during the middle of his program. He and his little sister had been taken out for dinner by their parents that evening, and after a big meal and a few hours in front of the TV, Thadius just couldn't keep his eyes open.

He groggily awoke when he was lifted off the sofa, believing his dad had picked him up to carry him to his bedroom, as he often did when the boy drifted off in front of his favorite programs. When he came round a little more, Thadius realized that he didn't recognize the teenager carrying out of his home. Trusting Thad assumed it was a family friend who'd woken him, and when Clark told the youngster he needed help to fix his broken car, the boy agreed to help, assuming the "family friend" didn't want to wake up his dad. When Clark told Thadius he should run alongside him toward the car, Thadius agreed. Little did he know, he was running towards the most painful, tortuous time of his life.

After running for about a mile, the pair made it to a dilapidated property, garbage strewn out the front of the unkempt building. When Clark told Thadius that was where he lived, the young boy felt his first pangs of uneasiness. Who is this person and why has he brought me here, Thad wondered. Entering the neglected house with the older boy he didn't recognize, Thadius knew something was wrong but followed instructions to make sure he didn't upset his abductor. As soon as the pair were inside, Clark forced a now-terrified Thadius up the stairs and threw him on the stained mattress in his bedroom.

He proceeded to grab the boy's ankle and twist it, turning it with such force that Thadius' ankle broke. When the cruel teenager eventually let go of Thad, the boy made a run for it despite the harsh injuries. Thadius would recall how he could feel the loose bones moving around his foot, saying the fear and confusion he felt helped him block out the pain. Sadly, Thadius wouldn't be able to avoid the pain for much longer since Clark was far from done with his victim.

Thad made it all the way downstairs before his attacker grabbed him from behind and dragged him into the living room. Here, he took Thadius' right leg, lifted it with as much force as he could over his head and pushed and pushed until the thigh eventually made a loud pop: it had snapped. The excruciating pain the teenager would have been in is almost unthinkable, let alone the emotional distress he was enduring throughout the ordeal. *Why was this happening to him? Who was his attacker? Would he ever see his family again?* Despite his broken bones, Thadius did everything he had to in order to survive, even if it meant befriending cruel Clark.

The pair even had normal conversations, talking about the usual things you'd expect two teen boys to chat about. Thadius eventually mustered up the courage to ask his attacker why he was doing this to him, and Clark replied that he enjoyed the sound of bones breaking. After thinking about his reply for a few moments, Thadius then asked Clark why he didn't just break his own bones in order to get his kicks. Surprisingly, Clark said he'd tried but couldn't get the angle right. Perhaps this statement is partially true, although some might guess that the reason he couldn't do it to himself is because the pain is too immense, not because of an issue with "angles."

A brief pause in the conversation was broken when Thadius asked his attacker if he'd ever done this to another boy before. "Yes," Clark replied. The conversation was over, and the night was just about over, too. The next day, Thadius asked his abductor if he could call his parents just to let them know he was okay. They'd surely be looking for him. To his surprise, Clark agreed, handing him the phone. Thadius tried calling with no luck since the phone was unplugged, and when he looked over at Clark, he saw he was laughing at him. It was a cruel joke, giving the victim some sense of hope when there wasn't any, then snatching it away for his sick pleasure. Thadius pleaded with the older boy to let him go, promising him he wouldn't tell a soul what had happened. He'd explain his injuries away as an accident, a nasty fall, or something. Clark scoffed at the idea, saying no one would believe his story. Freedom was getting further and further away from Thadius, and the young boy knew it.

That morning, the pair sat and watched TV in the living room. It wasn't long before Clark felt the urge to attack his victim again, so he took him upstairs and, this time, set about breaking his other ankle. He twisted so much that Thadius' foot was backward. Any screams or cries would only make Clark madder, and the attack would get more violent. The sadistic teen only seemed satisfied when he heard that sickening pop from breaking bones. When he was done with twisting Thadius' feet like they were made of rubber, he left him in agony on the bed. He'd run errands or try to fix his car, but it seemed like his rattletrap car not starting would enrage Clark so much he'd come back into the house and take his frustrations out on his vulnerable victim, sometimes jumping on the boy for fun.

When he was done, he'd put leg braces on Thadius and tell him to walk. He guided the boy to the top of the stairs and kicked him down, with the beaten boy left in a broken heap on the floor. Clark forced the boy back up into the bedroom and shut the door before heading out to see some friends.

This was Thadius' chance. As hard as it was to remain conscious, the determined boy dragged himself from the bedroom to the top of the stairs, flinging himself down until he again met the floor with an almighty crash. He knocked himself out on the way down, eating into the precious time he had to escape while Clark was out. Time passed, Thadius wasn't sure how much, but he awoke at the bottom of the stairs and began crawling through the living room, grit and determination fuelling his desire to get out and get home. Inch by inch, he was getting closer to freedom until he heard the door unlock. Clark was back. Thadius was dragged straight back up the stairs, and Clark's anger was unleashed on the barely conscious boy.

After twisting Thadius' limbs, his attacker would pull layer after layer of socks onto his twisted feet, meticulously ensuring the socks were aligned and the seams were straight and even. Clark had an unusual amount of brand-new white sports socks in his bedroom, with Thadius guessing his attacker had "hundreds" of pairs. Eventually, Thadius passed out due to the pain. When he awoke the next day, the pain was still unbearable, but the attacks were still relentless. Clark would use his knees on the boy's body, jumping as high as he could and landing knee-first onto Thadius. By the time he was done, Thadius' legs had swollen to twice their size, his feet weren't facing the right way, and his knee was broken. It would take a miracle for Thadius to put any weight on his legs.

As night time came around, Clark again headed out to see some friends. This gave Thadius another window of opportunity to escape if he could just stay conscious long enough to get to the kitchen and pull the phone down from the wall. However, Clark wasn't taking any chances with his captive, and when he set off for the evening, he made sure to lock Thadius inside his wardrobe. For some, this would be the moment where they'd give up. They'd assume they had no chance of escape, and even if they tried, they'd only end up getting tortured even more by their attacker. Not resilient Thadius, though. He rummaged through the dark wardrobe and looked for something to beat down the door with. Finding an old guitar, he summoned the strength to beat the door enough times to break it, eventually getting it open. Again, he had to throw himself down the stairs, and yet again, he landed at the bottom with a supreme crash. As before, he wound up unconscious.

Time passed as Thadius lay unresponsive on the cold floor. He awoke, and despite it being dark, he could just about work out where the phone was in the kitchen. He dragged himself there, reached up, pulled the cord so the phone fell with it, and dialed 911. He told the operator where he was and the name of his attacker. As soon as he said "Joe Clark," the dispatcher knew exactly what type of brute they were dealing with. Clark was well known to police with a lengthy criminal record, particularly for a 17-year-old boy. When police arrived at Clark's run-down torture house, they were shocked and sickened by the state they found Thadius in.

The boy was rushed to the hospital, mere hours away from death. If it wasn't for his inner strength, there's no doubt that Thad would have died that night. Not only did Thadius save his own life that night, but he also brought justice for the other boys Clark had brutally and fatally attacked. He told police straight away that he knew there had been other boys who'd been through this torture and recalled one of the victims was called Chris. As well as bringing justice to Clark's door,

Thadius also prevented other victims from meeting the same fate as him. Upon searching Clark's house, police found a hit list of young boys the twisted teen wanted to abuse. The list was titled, *"The Leg Thing."*

Clark pleaded no contest to the torture of Thadius. He was given a century behind bars for his evil crimes.

Still, it wasn't quite over. Police were looking into the other victims of Clark, and with Thadius calling one of them Chris, they connected it to the suspicious death of Chris Steiner just a year prior. The young boy was found submerged in water, having drowned to death after disappearing from his home in what appeared to be an abduction. Lack of evidence meant that the case had gone cold, but fresh hope had now arrived that the perpetrator could be brought to justice.

Chris' body was exhumed, and it was found his legs were broken in the same way Thadius' had been. The boy had been thrown into the river and was unable to swim due to his broken legs, causing him to drown. Such a cruel and terrifying way to die. Clarke denied - and still denies - Chris' murder, but he was found guilty of this cold-hearted killing, nonetheless.

Thadius had to endure several invasive surgeries after his ordeal and now walks with a limp; but he walks free, something that sick Clark will never do again.

The depravity of some human beings often defies belief: we simply can't comprehend that another human being would do this to another out of twisted pleasure. Clark knew what he was doing was wrong, hence the sneaky way he abducted his victims and kept them captive in order to carry out his acts of violence. He never intended for Thadius to survive the attacks. In fact, the night he was arrested, he was shocked to learn that Thadius was still alive. To Clark, leaving his victim to die alone in agony in the dark closet was perfectly reasonable. Should Thadius have met the same fate as Chris (and the other unknown boy whom Clark allegedly attacked), there would have been numerous other victims of Clark's twisted torture.

The idea that individuals like Clark walk among us is certainly chilling, but it's a sobering reminder that juvenile offenders can often be just as cruel and calculated as their adult counterparts. While Clark was just 17 when he was given life in jail, his vile acts and desire to break more bones was enough to strip him of his freedom. His lack of repentance and refusal to admit to other murders is what will keep him stripped of his liberty forever.

A Preventable Murder

Femicide and gender-based violence have become a heartbreaking mainstay in news headlines. In the UK, the case of Sarah Everard caused an uproar when she went missing in the spring of 2021. On the fateful night of March 3, 2021, 33-year-old Sarah Everard was walking home alone from a friend's house in South London. Little did she know that her life would be cut short in an instant by an off-duty police officer, Wayne Couzens. The depraved, crooked cop stopped her, identifying himself as a police officer, before handcuffing her and placing her in his car. He then took her on a terrifying journey near Dover, where he subjected her to rape and strangled her to death. Couzens then burned her body and disposed of her remains in a nearby pond.

While Couzens got life behind bars for his abhorrent crime, Sarah's murder sparked a nationwide debate about the role of police in society and the safety of women in the UK.

In the USA, Gabby Petito's American dream of traveling across the United States with her fiancé Brian Laundrie turned into a true American nightmare. The 22-year-old was murdered by her partner during their stint at experiencing "van life" together. Gabby vanished in late August 2021, casting heavy suspicion over Laundrie when he drove their van back to Florida alone with not so much as a word about his fiancé's whereabouts.

Laundrie left his home on September 13 and was reported missing four days later.

By September 19, the worst outcome emerged: Gabby's remains were found in Wyoming's Bridger-Teton National Forest. The cause of death was strangulation. After a month of searching for Laundrie, his remains were finally discovered in Florida's Myakkahatchee Creek Environmental Park on October 20. It was later confirmed that he had taken his own life with a self-inflicted gunshot to the head. In a heartbreaking twist, the FBI revealed that Laundrie had confessed to killing Gabby in a notebook found near his remains.

Both of these tragic cases are recent examples of femicide, and both of these crimes received a high level of press coverage. The outrage and shock these cases caused had a ripple effect across the mainstream press and social media, and each case had core aspects that people were talking about. Sarah Everard's case had people questioning the police and their trustworthiness. Gabby Petito's case covered the domestic abuse incidents that plagued their toxic relationship. The case I'm about to cover, the murder of Shana Grice, encases both of these elements. The person who ended her life was her abusive ex, whom she'd reported to police multiple times. The police didn't just dismiss the 19-year-old's claims - they fined her for wasting police time. This gave 27-year-old Michael Lane the opportunity to end his teenage ex-girlfriend's life in a most cruel way.

Shana was described as being outgoing and peppy. She grew up just outside of Brighton with her parents, Richard and Sharon. The couple doted on their only child, who grew up to be hard-working and independent. Despite being young, the teen took on a job at a fire alarm installation business in order to help save for her dream wedding to childhood sweetheart, Ashley Cooke. The pair had been together since meeting at high school, and it was assumed by all that they'd end up marrying and starting a family, eventually. However, there was a spanner thrown in the works for this fairytale when Shana met mechanic Michael Lane at work.

She made it clear she was in a relationship, but that didn't put Michael off. The attraction was there, and Michael was persistent. Eventually, an affair ensued, and Shana and her new lover were secretly meeting behind Ashley's back. The romance was filled with ups and downs, and Shana and Michael would often break it off before reconciling.

Michael wouldn't take the final break-up well. In fact, he didn't take any of their breaks particularly well, but when she ended it for good, he ramped up his nefarious ways. In the months prior to her tragic and brutal murder, Shana went to the police numerous times about her former love interest. Michael Lane had been spying on his obsession by monitoring the tracker he covertly placed on her vehicle. Every movement Shana made pinged straight through to Michael's phone. To know the depths his jealousy and malice would later go, this is a particularly chilling part of the case. The jilted ex would know where his object of desire was and, in all probability, turn up just to spy on Shana.

In February 2016, Shana was fed up with Michael's unwanted advances and inability to accept rejection. Her car had been vandalized, and she'd been receiving flowers from him despite her insistence their relationship was over. He'd also been loitering around her house despite being told the relationship was over. Shana called the police and made a complaint about her ex harassing her. Crucially, in this call, she told police, "I think I'm being stalked." Nothing came of this, but the following month, she had to call the police on Michael again.

In March 2016, Michael assaulted Shana, snatching her phone from her and grabbing a fist of her hair, which resulted in the abusive man being arrested on suspicion of assault. In a twist of injustice, not only was Michael allowed to walk away without any charges being brought toward him, but the police fined Shana for wasting police time. Her crime? She did not disclose the fact she'd been in a relationship with

Michael. She was ordered to pay £90 for this indiscretion, although with Shana now back with her childhood sweetheart, you can see why she didn't want to draw attention to her affair. In a lack of good practice, Shana was interviewed by police about her stalker in front of her partner Ashley, so the hesitancy to explain the relationship is understandable. If she'd been taken to one side and spoken to, perhaps she could have revealed more, and this tale could have ended differently.

Still, why her omission would warrant a fine is beyond me, let alone the fact the real culprit in this crime was allowed to walk away without so much as a warning.

However, when someone is obsessed, there's little a warning would do. It appears this is where Sussex Police failed Shana time and time again: by not recognizing the fact that she was being stalked. Stalking is often fueled by obsession toward the victim, and Shana wasn't safeguarded from her stalker despite multiple attempts to apprehend him.

A few months later, in July 2016, Michael made use of Shana's spare key to her home. She hadn't given him the key willingly; he'd stolen it from her. If she'd known he'd been carrying around a key to her property, there's no doubt she'd have changed the locks and invested in some security cameras for her home.

On a warm summer night, Michael used her key, crept up her stairs, and stood over her while she was asleep in bed. However, Shana wasn't asleep. She was wide awake, and her heart was pounding underneath the covers. She knew it was her unpredictable, abusive ex hovering over her, and she thought if she pretended to be asleep, he'd not harm her. She'd heard him enter the house, and his footsteps gave him away. After standing over her for what felt like an eternity to Shana, Michael eventually vacated the property.

When she heard the front door close, Shana felt safe enough to peek out of her bedroom window. Not that she needed confirmation who the intruder was: she saw Michael walking away from her home and called the police.

This time, Michael was given a police caution. They told him to stay away from his ex, although again when someone is obsessed, a simple slap on the wrists isn't going to deter them. Michael wasn't apprehended for stalking or breaking and entering, though; he was arrested for theft. No mention of stalking or Michael's previous obsessive behavior towards Shana was noted.

In fact, just one day after being told to leave Shana alone, the teenager began to receive phone calls from an unknown number. The caller didn't speak when Shana answered; they just breathed heavily. She ignored most of the no-caller ID calls but made sure to contact police and let them know that Michael was breaching his caution. This didn't do much, however. Police advised they'd make a note of the complaint and leave it on file, but they didn't pay a visit to Michael despite his continuous stalking of Shana.

Just days after this, Shana was yet again forced to call the police when she was being tailed by Michael, but there was no action taken against him.

The following month saw Michael strike again. In August 2016, Shana was at home with her friend when her stalker appeared right outside her property. This time, she had a witness to corroborate her story that Michael was loitering despite being told to stay away. But she was too afraid to go to the police this time, even with her friend there to confirm the truth. Shana was scared that she would be dismissed again and was fearful she'd be slapped with another £90 fine for wasting police time.

It seemed Shana felt defeated by this point. The fact she'd been fined had been a crushing blow to her, and she didn't feel like she was believed. Because her relationship with Michael had been an affair, she felt like she was being judged morally and that it looked like she was lying. With Shana feeling like she couldn't rely on the police to ensure her stalker kept away from her, she enlisted the help of family and friends, making sure they knew to check in with her if she hadn't spoken to them for a few hours.

Meanwhile, Michael was also enlisting the help of friends to listen to his sob story of being dumped. "She'll pay for what she's done," the bitter man told a friend about Shana rekindling things with her boyfriend. These sinister words were perhaps taken as Michael letting off steam about his love life, but retrospectively, he meant those words with every fiber of his being.

Later that month, on August 25, Michael yet again went to Shana's property. He broke in and again crept up to Shana's room. This time, he wouldn't just stand over her. He brought a knife and sliced her throat. Satisfied with his act of violent brutality, he set fire to her bedroom before fleeing the scene. The 19-year-old was found by her partner's dad, Ian Cooke.

Police honed in on Michael Lane as soon as they were informed of the sadistic killing. Surprisingly, he told police he was at Shana's house that day but insisted she was already dead when he got there. Fearful he'd be blamed if he called for help, he panicked and left without telling anybody about the murder of his ex-girlfriend. Michael's tall tale was about as believable as the tooth fairy, and he was charged with Shana Grice's murder. In March 2017, he was found guilty and was handed life in jail, with a minimum of 25 years behind bars.

This case is undeniably frustrating. The senseless murder of a young woman was thoroughly preventable due to the amount of times she flagged Michael's actions to the police, and their handling of her situation was undoubtedly lackluster. The judge sentencing Michael said at his trial, "You were treated as the victim," adding that those investigating had "no appreciation on the part of those investigating that a young woman in a sexual relationship with a man could, at the same time, be vulnerable and at risk of serious harm."

A two-year investigation into the way Shana's case was dealt with ensued. Members of staff were investigated for misconduct, and two were looked into for gross misconduct. The officer who spoke to Shana in front of her boyfriend was found guilty of misconduct by not delving into Shana's grievance that she was being stalked and harassed by Michael Lane. The other officer accused of gross misconduct had since retired.

To top this off, it was revealed that it wasn't just Shana who had contacted authorities to complain about Michael's unwanted attention and disturbing behaviors. A total of 13 women had been to the police prior to Shana. It was found Lane had harassed various girls between 2006 and 2016 and had even been arrested in 2010 for grooming a young girl while he worked as a scout leader. While there were never any charges brought on from his arrest, the grooming allegation was still on his record.

It was also uncovered that Michael Lane had a pattern of consistent controlling behavior toward his partners, all of which run parallel to the harassment he bestowed upon Shana. From unwanted explicit texts to standing outside their property to sexual assault, Lane had been accused of many vile acts of control prior to his final act of control on Shana.

Every murder is tragic, but ones like this are so easily avoidable that you can't help feeling that extra pang of frustration about it. While the police are there to protect and serve, cases like this remind me of just how important it is to remain vigilant.

The Sadistic Student

The last thing you imagine a 14-year-old could be is a cold-blooded killer.

Thinking back to 14-year-old you, you may recall just finding your feet at high school (or perhaps you were like me, not finding your feet for years after high school), or you will perhaps remember dying your hair for the first time or even that age being the first time you got tipsy from raiding your parent's alcohol cupboard. Whatever you think back to, I'm sure it's memories filled with innocence and teen angst, even the memories where your behavior wasn't the greatest. Your teen years are your experimental years, the time when you're desperately trying to find your place and figure out who you are. Some kids are still playing with toys at the age of 14, which makes this case even harder to digest.

For ninth-grader Philip Chism, at age 14, he was plotting rape and murder. Worse still, he carried out his twisted fantasy on October 22, 2013. The object of his warped desires was his teacher, Colleen Ritzer.

Colleen was a well-liked teacher at Danvers High School in Massachusetts, perhaps due to being one of the younger tutors at just 24 years old. Always keen to help out when students needed some assistance to understand their math homework, Colleen pinpointed Philip as someone who needed some extra guidance. On that fateful October day, the kind teacher had unknowingly stepped into her depraved student's twisted trap.

Philip, born January 1999, was somewhat of an outcast at school. He'd only just arrived at Danvers High School after moving from Tennessee, but he hadn't made much of an impact when it came to making new friends. While he was good on the soccer pitch, he didn't seem to mesh well enough with the team to form any bonds with his fellow players. In fact, he was described as being anti-social, often coming across to others as tired and not really present when having a conversation. This may, in part, have been due to difficulties at home. His mother was going through a divorce at the time, a stressful situation that could well have affected Philip's desire to socialize.

In stark contrast to Philip's insular, loner persona, Colleen was peppy, engaging, and happy to talk to anyone. One of her students would later say of her former math teacher, "She made me feel like I wanted to go to math class," a phrase that I doubt is often used when it comes to the subject of mathematics (speaking from personal experience, anyhow). It was clear to see that Colleen was well-regarded by her students and made time for each of them, including Philip.

At one point, Colleen saw Philip's sketches in his workbook and complimented the teen on his artistic talents. It seemed she had managed to prise some conversation out of the teen until she mentioned his move from Tennessee. Then his mood turned sour. Visibly agitated about the topic, Philip retreated back into himself while Colleen tried to steer the conversation in another direction. However, it seemed it was too late: the flustered boy was clearly upset. Other students noticed he began chattering away to himself.

On the day of the murder, Philip was caught on the school's CCTV walking towards his locker with a number of bags and stacking them inside. There was no way anyone could know what was inside his bags. A mask and gloves, various items of clothing, and a box cutter were among his belongings. Philip had been planning this for a while, and today was the day his sadistic fantasy came true.

While carrying out her after-class tutoring, Colleen stepped out of the classroom to use the bathroom. Philip felt this was his chance. He got out of his seat and tailed the young teacher's footsteps. CCTV catches him following her, then stopping. It could have been he was second-guessing his acts, or he was considering that this wasn't the right time to carry out his planned attack. Either way, he decided to proceed with his plan. He pulled his hood over his head for whatever reason; it didn't matter, since CCTV had already caught a clear as day image of his face. The camera caught the teen pulling some latex gloves out of his pocket and putting them on before following Colleen into the restroom.

He cornered the young woman before robbing her of her phone, credit cards, and forcing her to hand over her underwear. Box cutter in hand, Philip raped her before stabbing his teacher almost 20 times in her neck. The fatal wound was a slicing of her artery from behind. It was a brutal and gruesome killing that was almost witnessed firsthand when a student entered the restroom as the crime was occurring. The female student noticed a pile of crumpled clothing on the floor, spotting someone unclothed, and quickly exited the restroom to give the person more privacy to get changed. In reality, it was Colleen's lifeless body she'd seen. The clothes on the floor had been forcibly removed from her.

Cameras showed Philip had been in the bathroom with Colleen for just over 10 minutes when he emerged from the crime scene. He didn't stay away, however. He came back a few minutes later, pulling a recycling bin with a brand new outfit on.

CCTV captured Philip returning to his victim with the bin, where he dumped her body, before donning a ski mask and pulling her corpse out of the building. It's unclear what Philip thought he was doing by changing his clothes so often. Not only had he been caught on camera, his costume changes were blatant and did little to disguise his identity.

Around an hour after the horrific attack on Colleen, Philip was again caught on the school's security cameras, yet again in fresh clothing, at his locker and loitering around the murder scene.

The killer didn't go home after school as he normally would. Instead, he took himself off to the cinema, courtesy of Colleen's credit card. His worried mother had no option but to call the police when her son didn't return home. After all, he had no friends who she could contact and ask his whereabouts, and she knew he was a lone wolf at school who was unlikely to have been invited to a social gathering. The police eventually found Philip brooding along a busy highway in the early hours of October 23.

There was no resistance from the teen when police searched the boy, whose hands were still bloodied from his killing hours earlier. A look inside his bag saw police find the box cutter, also still bloodied. The officers asked where all the blood was from, likely not expecting Philip's monotone answer. "The girl," he said.

A further look inside the boy's macabre bag of horrors revealed he had a pair of women's underwear and a collection of credit cards belonging to a female. It seemed like the police had unknowingly happened upon a callous killer.

Meanwhile, Colleen's family was also panicked that she'd not returned home. Again, it was most unusual for her. For her to just stay out and not contact anyone was beyond out of character, so a missing person's report was filed for her on the night of October 22. Shortly after this, her body was found in the woods close to the school. Her mutilated corpse was found to be staged suggestively, and disturbingly, the culprit had also violated Colleen with tree branches that had to be removed from her. Not far from the body, investigators found a neatly folded note that read, "I hate you all."

As part of the investigation, the police obtained the CCTV from Danvers High School to trace Colleen's steps. It was around the time Philip was detained by police that the footage was viewed, making him a suspect. Once it was ascertained he was found with Colleen's belongings and a bloodied box cutter it seemed their worst fears had been realized.

Philip Chism told police everything - except why he carried out the sickening crime.

When he turned 16, he was tried as an adult for the murder. His defense saw him admit to the murder of Colleen but claimed that he wasn't mentally well enough to be considered responsible for the killing. Philip had insisted he'd been hearing voices prior to carrying out the crime, and his attorney said a psychotic episode was to blame for his violent outburst.

However, he was eventually convicted of raping Colleen prior to murdering her but was acquitted of a second sexual assault allegation pertaining to the violation with the branch. He was found guilty of armed robbery for the theft of Colleen's credit cards and underwear. When the verdicts were read out to him, Philip showed no emotion. He looked at the judge like you look at a shopkeeper when paying for your gas. There was nothing there; no guilt, no remorse, no disgust for himself, not even any sorrow for himself. There was one person in the courtroom who was visibly full of emotion, though: his mother, Diana. To know your son is capable of carrying out such a sadistic and brutal attack must be an earth-shattering realization. While they say a mother's love is unconditional, to ever look at your boy in the same way would be near impossible.

Upon leaving the courthouse, Diana declined requests to talk to reporters.

Colleen's parents were in attendance, too, although the guilty verdict gave them no sense of victory or closure. Her father, Thomas, spoke of his daughter's senseless murder and reiterated that although her killer was behind bars for now, he will be eligible for parole in 40 years' time. Philip, still a teenager, would have enough time to start life afresh at that point, albeit in middle age. For Colleen, middle age is a milestone that was stripped from her out of a sadistic young boy's lust.

The Lonely Hearts Killers

Killer couples are an interesting subcategory of true crime, perhaps because it entwines both love and a lust for murder: two polar opposites that collide to create truly macabre results.

The ability to love another person does not abolish the ability - or desire - to murder another person, even though we often view killers as cold, unfeeling creatures. The scary part is that a lot of them are not. In the case of Raymond Martinez Fernandez and his common-law wife, Martha Jule Beck, the love they had for one another knew no bounds, especially for Martha. Not only would she jump at Raymond's every whim, but she would kill for (and with) him.

The tale began in Hawaii in 1914. Raymond Fernandez was born here to Spanish parents, who were reportedly disappointed by their son's perpetually sickly appearance. It was his father, in particular, who was resentful of the boy, wishing the couple had a tougher child with a stronger air about him. The boy was well aware of the disdain his father held for him, and when the family moved to Connecticut in 1932, Raymond quickly decided to flee the family unit and live with his uncle in Spain.

By this point, the once-frail boy was now a healthy-looking young man, and he soon married a young woman called Encarnacion. The couple had four children, but marital bliss wouldn't be on the cards for too long.

World War II saw young Raymond work with the Spanish Merchant Marine, but he was quickly picked up by Britain to work as a spy. By all accounts, his ability to covertly gather information was admirable, and he was good at his job. When the war ended, Raymond chose not to return to Spain and set sail for America instead. His initial plan was to set up home in the U.S., then send for his wife and kids. However, an accident on the ship headed to the States would change Raymond's life forever.

While making his way to the deck, a steel hatch came loose and landed on his head, causing an awful injury, both externally and causing permanent damage to his brain. He was bed-bound in the hospital for almost four months. Upon his release, he wasn't the same man he was before the accident. His moods were constantly sour. He was quick to erupt into a rage, and rarely did he manage to crack a smile. It's been well-documented that head trauma can trigger a change in personality when a person takes damage to their frontal lobe area, which is precisely where Raymond suffered his damage.

The mild-mannered family man was no longer, and Raymond was now driven by impulse and desire, not by reason or logic.

This was first shown when he tried to board another ship after being discharged from the hospital. Raymond had long forgotten his family by this point, and any plan to move them to America with him was quickly dropped. While passing through customs, he took it upon himself to enter a luggage room for the ship and take hordes of clothing and items that belonged to other passengers. Perhaps if Raymond had picked up one or two items, he might have gotten away with the crime, but he decided to stuff garment after garment into his bag. He was stopped by customs and sent to jail for a year in Florida for this thievery. It was here he'd meet a man who'd change his way of thinking, a fellow criminal who delved into voodoo. Raymond's cellmate told of all the ways this black magic can give you immense power over women, and the idea of sexual persuasion intrigued him.

He spent his time in jail reading up on his new obsession, believing he could gain control over women from afar by inserting "voodoo" into letters he sent to them. All he'd need is a lock of their hair, or failing that, an item that belonged to the woman, and he could carry out a ritual that would render them his.

When he was released in 1946, Raymond would be sure to make full use of his new "abilities." With nowhere to live, he moved in with his sister. Her Brooklyn home proved spacious enough for the pair of them, although with no job it was unclear to Raymond's sister how he would contribute to paying the bills: he had a plan, however.

Almost as soon as he unpacked his clothes, he set about writing letter after letter to women from the lonely heart columns of various newspapers. Soon enough, the replies flooded in and Raymond corresponded with them all. He gained these women's trust, arranged to meet them, and would then flee with their money and jewelry. His victims would feel too ashamed to report Raymond's cruel crimes to the police, allowing the callous man to carry on duping woman after woman.

One woman, however, managed to escape Raymond's meet-and-fleece scheme. She didn't manage to make it out alive, though. Her name was Jane Thompson, and like the others, she was lonely and vulnerable. The pair met up, bought some tickets for a cruise to Spain, and took off together. They traveled the picturesque countryside in the warm weather and even booked their hotel rooms as a married couple. It's unclear if Raymond had told his new love interest that he was already married, but it wouldn't take long for Jane to find out. It was Raymond himself who introduced his mistress and his wife when he passed by his old home in La Linea. The two women seemed to get on with one another, and the three would often be seen eating out together and walking through town.

The situation took a sinister turn on a November night in 1947. Raymond and Jane had an argument in their hotel room, with Raymond seen fleeing the area after their nasty confrontation. Perhaps he's heading off to cool down, people may have wondered. But he didn't return to the hotel, and the next morning, Jane was found dead in their room. By this point, Raymond was well on his way out of the country, leaving not only his wife and children for the second time, but also a dead body.

Jane's body wasn't autopsied, and her cause of death wasn't clear.

Back in the safety of New York, Raymond picked up where he left off with the lonely hearts columns. He wrote to dozens upon dozens of women, and one in particular took a keen interest in her new pen pal. Her name was Martha Seabrook.

Martha was born in 1919 in Florida. As she was growing up, she matured faster than the rest of the girls her age. She had a young woman's body by the age of ten and showed overt sexual tendencies for a young child. She was also overweight for her age and stature. These were all symptoms of a glandular condition Martha suffered from, although this didn't stop the kids in her class from mocking and ridiculing her. It seemed there was no respite from the bullying when Martha was at home, either, since her mother treated her with disdain and contempt. It came to light, after Martha's arrest years later, that she was sexually abused by her brother. When she went to her mother for help as a youngster, her cruel parent beat her up, blaming the child for the abuse she'd endured. It's no surprise, then, that Martha was a shy, reclusive child with no friends.

As she grew older, her weight gain prevented her from being a nurse, the only career she'd ever dreamed of doing. Instead, she found work embalming bodies at a funeral home. Working alone with dead people couldn't have done much for Martha's ability to socialize, but at least there wasn't any danger of being ridiculed by the corpses she was preparing for burial.

Soon, the lifestyle she was living became too lonely to bear. Martha moved to sunny California in search of pastures new, and she picked up work in the Army hospital, finally holding the job title she'd always longed for: Nurse Martha. Her line of work meant she was surrounded by soldiers on a regular basis, and would often sleep with them, although rarely did one ever see her for more than one encounter. It was after a sneaky meeting with a soldier that Martha fell pregnant. Overjoyed, Martha told the father-to-be the good news. He responded by trying to kill himself.

Humiliated, depressed, and soon to be an unwed mother, Martha headed back to Florida. She couldn't tell those that knew her the truth, so she lied and said she was newly married and that the father of her child was going to join her in Florida as soon as he could. To end this lie, or cover it up, she eventually told people her husband had been killed at war, convincing people with her hysterical crying.

Her daughter was born in 1944, and that same year, she got pregnant again. She married the child's father, Alfred Beck, but he divorced her barely six months later. Alone with two small kids to support, Martha was again at a low ebb. To pull herself out of the depressive state she was sinking into, she placed an advert in "Mother Dinene's Family Club for Lonely Hearts." It gave her something to get up for, to see if there was anything exciting in the mailbox from a potential suitor. Weeks passed, until one day, she awoke to a letter from a Mr Raymond Fernandez. Martha was giddy with excitement.

Raymond said he was a wealthy business owner. He was polite and well-mannered, he was exotic, and he was on the lookout for a wife. For Martha, he was *the one*. After the giddiness subsided, Martha suddenly felt a pang of dread: what if Raymond was put off by her size? After receiving a photo of Raymond, she sent one back but made sure to send a flattering one where her body was hidden by the other people in the photo. She made sure to note in her letter that the enclosed picture didn't do her justice.

Eventually, Raymond asked for a lock of Martha's hair, something he made sure to request from all his pen pals. He used it to perform his voodoo prior to meeting them. While some may have found this an odd request and decline to snip off their hair, Martha was thrilled she'd been asked for something so intimate and spritzed her locks with perfume before slipping them into an envelope. As soon as the hair was delivered to Raymond, he carried out his ritual. Now, it was time to meet.

Despite Martha being anxious that she'd told a few fibs about her true appearance, the pair met in December 1947. Raymond took the train to visit his latest victim, and upon seeing Martha, a smile of pure joy lit up his face. To her relief, it seemed Raymond didn't care about Martha's white lies, and the pair enjoyed dinner at her place. She introduced her kids to her new man but ushered them to bed as soon as she could so she could have more one-on-one time with Raymond.

After spending the night together, Raymond spent several days with Martha. She jumped to his every request while he spent the time scoping out whether the woman had any assets of value or he'd simply wasted his time meeting her. He must have come to the conclusion that Martha had nothing to fleece as he abruptly told her he had to go back to New York quickly to tend to work. After he left, he wrote to Martha and told her he wouldn't be seeing her again. She was heartbroken. So much so, she tried to end her life. After informing Raymond of this, he begrudgingly let her visit him in New York. She would return to Florida after two weeks, pick up her kids, and land on Raymond's doorstep, much to his dismay.

At best, this was an inconvenience. How could he continue his lucrative business with Martha and her kids running about? He gave the woman an ultimatum: either they all go, or the kids go. She marched the children to the Salvation Army and returned to Raymond child-free. Perhaps as a way to scare her off, Raymond told Martha about his lonely heart fleecing business and pulled out a thick stack of letters he'd received from all his other women. It didn't matter. Martha told him she would stick by him no matter what. That night, they sat down and picked out a new victim.

Esther Henne had been speaking to Raymond for weeks. The pair met up in early 1948, with the charming man bringing his sister-in-law to the first meeting. This was, in fact, Martha, who had to idly stand by and watch her lover court an infatuated Esther over the next few weeks. Eventually, once they'd swindled the woman for hundreds of dollars, she became spooked by their treatment of her and fled a once-adoring Raymond and his cold sister-in-law.

The next victim was a woman named Myrtle Young, who Raymond married. Martha did all she could to put a stop to the newlyweds' ever getting intimate, something that became apparent to young Myrtle. Martha insisted the new bride didn't sleep in the marital bed but that she sleep with her instead, which Myrtle begrudgingly agreed with. When she was alone with Raymond, Martha would moan and cry about the third woman in the relationship, something that would frustrate Raymond. To end her nagging, he drugged Myrtle one evening and carried her onto a bus going to Arkansas. The sheer amount of drugs she'd been plied with meant that Myrtle never made it out of her slumber, and she died the following day.

The couple continued their nefarious business, taking what they could from unsuspecting women looking for a life partner. In December 1948, the pair met up with Janet Fay, a well-off woman from New York. Martha was introduced as Raymond's sister and yet again had to endure watching the man she loved woo another woman. Janet and Raymond married quickly after meeting, and Raymond wasn't shy about dipping into Janet's bank accounts at will.

Having to put on a poker face every time she saw Janet and Raymond being affectionate was beginning to become too much for Martha to bear. She was seething with envy, and her resentment towards her unknowing love rival was hitting dangerous levels. This became apparent to Janet, who eventually asked her new husband's strange sister to leave the marital home. This enraged Martha beyond belief. Martha grabbed a hammer and bludgeoned the woman over the head until she fell to the floor. The incensed woman then grabbed a nearby scarf and strangled Janet to death.

Notifying Raymond of the murder, he didn't scold her for losing her temper. Instead, he helped his partner in crime bundle Janet into some towels before locking her in the wardrobe. That night, Martha got what she'd been longing for: a night in Raymond's bed.

The murderous pair ended up putting Janet's corpse in a trunk and burying it underneath the basement of a house they rented. Raymond made sure to rinse the remaining money in his dead wife's accounts and made sure to cover up the crime as best he could. He typed up a letter to Janet's family pretending to be her, telling them she was moving to Florida. This plan could have worked if Raymond had gotten to know his wife better: Janet couldn't work a typewriter and didn't know how to type. Police were called about the suspicious letter.

Meanwhile, the sinister duo were back to their lonely hearts' swindle. The next victim was a single mother-of-one, Delphine Downing, whom Raymond quickly swept off her feet. Yet again, Martha was seething that the man she loved was sleeping with another woman right in front of her. She couldn't let it show, though, since she was again introduced as Raymond's clingy, unbearable sister.

While Delphine was initially impressed by Raymond, she soon discovered he wore a toupee and, upon seeing him without his wig, became unattracted to her lover. She told Raymond as much, too, something he tried to overcome with his charm and desperate words of affection. Delphine felt duped, and things began to get heated.

Martha stepped in and gave the distressed woman some sleeping tablets. This helped pacify Delphine, who soon fell into a slumber. However, her baby girl began to cry, and without her mother there to comfort her, Martha headed over to the cot instead. She didn't soothe the little girl. She choked her instead.

The brutal attack left visible bruises on the baby's neck, something that angered Raymond: how could he explain this to Delphine when she eventually came around? There was only one solution. She had to die.

Raymond shot Delphine in the head with her own gun as she slept. The pair dumped her body in the basement and cemented over the makeshift grave they'd made. It only took the killers a few days to empty Delphine's bank accounts and cash in any checks they found. The baby girl was still alive, although it was a big inconvenience for the pair. She cried. Nothing would pacify her. She needed attention, and she wouldn't eat. Raymond insisted Martha kill her. They carried the crying baby to the basement where her mother's body had been buried and filled a nearby metal container full of water. Martha held the girl underwater and drowned her.

Meanwhile, locals were becoming suspicious that they'd not seen Delphine for a while. They went to the police about their concerns, and authorities turned up at Delphine's house to see if anything sinister had been going on.

It didn't take the police long to arrest the soon-to-be-named lonely heart killers.

Raymond was the first to stand trial in 1949, telling the jury how Martha killed Janet. He also retracted his initial confession of any murders, stating he was just trying to protect his loved one. Martha sat and looked up as Raymond heaped the blame onto her, nodding in agreement, still doing anything her man asked her to. When the prosecution went in on Raymond, Martha stood up and yelled in his defense despite her lover turning against her. He insisted that he had taken the heat because he would've handled jail better than his female accomplice, perhaps trying to prove to the jury he was a gentleman simply caught up with a crazed murderer.

When Martha eventually took the stand, nobody knew how it would pan out. Would she take all the blame, or would she point the finger at Raymond? She said she couldn't recall much of the night Janet was killed, telling the jury she awoke from a blackout to Raymond shouting at her as she stood over the dead woman's body. She told the court how "a request from Mr. Fernandez to me is a command" and gushed about her love for him.

Ultimately, the pair were sentenced to the electric chair, set to be carried out that year.

While they awaited imminent death, the pair sat behind bars, and a surprise back-and-forth emanated from the lovers. Raymond accused his lover of engaging in an illicit affair with a prison guard, something Martha denied. She told the press Raymond was destroying the little decency she had left and scoffed at his reported desire to be put to death early. He'd never willingly die, Martha said, although he can easily take the life of another human being. Her support of him seemed to be slipping. She called him a lying rat and a double-crosser.

While Martha was reeling about Raymond's accusations, he was writing to his first wife, declaring his love for her and their children. Long-suffering Encarnacion was won round by her husband's charm and reciprocated his words of love.

March 8, 1949, was Martha and Raymond's execution date. She requested eggs, ham, and a coffee as her last breakfast. Her last evening meal was a pile of fried chicken, a smattering of fries on the side, with an accompanying salad. Raymond had an omelet and a cigar.

Tradition at Sing Sing prison was for the weakest out of a criminal duo to be put to death first. Raymond was called upon first. He was led from his cell to the chair. He dropped to the floor, needing to be carried by guards. He told the crowd-watching that he loved Martha before being pronounced dead minutes later. Martha walked to the chair of her own accord, although some matrons accompanied her at her request. She whispered, "So long," before electricity was pumped into her body.

This twisted tale of passion and murder is a prevalent theme in true crime cases. Often, there is a clear, uneven power dynamic in killer couples; one of them has an unhealthy control over the other, who in turn is eager to do whatever they have to in order to please their partner. This doesn't abolish the often-codependent person in the relationship, though: think of the crimes Myra Hindley took part in with her boyfriend Ian Brady. From going along with his twisted fantasies to carrying out horrifically brutal acts on children to please him, she dove to sadistic depths to maintain her relationship with Brady.

Then there's the sickening case of Karla Homolka and Paul Bernardo, who together kidnapped and raped women and children, recording their sick crimes on camera. While Karla was a victim of Paul's aggression, often sporting black eyes and bust lips from his hands, that didn't stop her from saying yes when Paul suggested they rape her sister together. Tragically, Karla's sister died the night they attacked her. The duo got it all on camera, too.

When you delve under the surface of killer couples, it truly is a terrifying thought. This twisted dynamic often means the duo have a strong (albeit toxic) bond where they manipulate and control each other. The idea of two people committing such atrocities together is especially chilling because it offers us a different level of depravity and evil that's difficult for us to understand. Can you imagine what you'd do if your spouse came to you and told you about the murderous desires they were harboring?

36 Hours Of Hell

Few crimes make you as angry as those that involve a child. While in the case I'm about to cover, it was a 30-year-old woman who was the victim of a brutal crime, she had the mind of a child. The heartbreaking naivety and innocence Jennifer Daugherty displayed before and during her senseless murder makes this torture-killing all the more harrowing.

Jennifer had a learning disability that rendered her, in essence, a child for life. This meant she had the innate excitement and curiosity of a youngster, but it also meant she was incredibly trusting. Kids tend not to see the bad in people or recognize danger when it presents itself, and Jennifer was no different. Still, the woman lived a relatively independent life with the support of her family. She'd often hop on the bus from her home in Mount Pleasant, Pennsylvania, to the city of Greensburg to run errands.

Jennifer had hopes of getting her own home, getting married and having a family of her own one day, and she was becoming increasingly self-sufficient in order to make this dream a reality. Prior to her murder, Jennifer was getting ready to climb the career ladder to help make her lifestyle dreams come true and was training to become a mechanic.

She felt optimistic about her future, and her last social media post reflected this, writing that she was intending to "make new friends and not be afraid of anything."

While Jennifer was surrounded by an abundance of love from her mother, stepdad, and other members of her family, she endured a cold and lonely existence outside of the family circle. Although she was bullied and tormented throughout school, a set of close friends was something she still desperately wanted. This undoubtedly made it easier for her killers to befriend her - although I use the term befriend loosely - and carry out their 36-hour torture of naïve Jennifer.

While on one of her many bus trips to Greensburg, Jennifer went to the West Place Clubhouse, a drop-in center for people struggling with their mental health. The center offered a safe space for diagnosed individuals to get help with seeking employment and integrating themselves into working life. It was here she would make friends with her soon-to-be killers. In particular, she was friendly with 17-year-old Angela Marinucci, who also frequented the Clubhouse. Angela suffered a head injury when she was younger, resulting in permanent cognitive impairment, and used the Clubhouse to socialize and make use of their computers.

The pair became fast friends, frequently talking on the phone and arranging meet-ups at West Place. It was through Angela that Jennifer came to know and befriend Ricky Smyrnes, who was also Angela's boyfriend. Ricky didn't have the best upbringing, with various stints in numerous foster homes, causing him to turn to alcohol and drugs at an incredibly young age. It's been reported he'd had his first taste of hardcore drugs at the heartbreaking age of six before being placed with the Smyrnes family at age ten. While his new home offered stability, it seemed like this was a foreign concept to young Ricky, and he resorted to a life of petty crimes and drugs.

He did some time behind bars, where he would become friends with Melvin Knight, a fellow convict who would also be introduced to Jennifer. In turn, Melvin introduced his girlfriend, Amber Medinger, to Jennifer, as well as their other friends from the West Place Clubhouse, Robert Masters and Peggy Miller. All six of Jennifer's newfound friends had either cognitive or learning difficulties.

On February 10, 2010, Jennifer's step dad drove her to the bus station as he regularly did. She liked to get around on her own and enjoyed the bus route to Greensburg. This time, she was making her way to Angela's home for a sleepover. This was something Jennifer had been longing for her whole life: a friend who she could confide in, someone who would enjoy spending time with her and who didn't offer cruel judgment. Jennifer's plan was to spend the night at her new best friend's house, then head to Greensburg the following morning as she often liked to do. Before she accepted the offer of a lift from her step dad, she quickly jotted a note on the back of an envelope for her mother. It read, "*I love you very much. I will talk to you sometime later.*"

Sometime later would never arrive.

Excited about the sleepover, Jennifer hopped off the bus. She was overwhelmed with joy at the idea she now had a friendship group and couldn't wait to meet up with them. Eventually, she made her way to Angela's place, although Jennifer's new friends weren't exactly excited to have her around. Unbeknown to her, they were plotting something violent and sinister.

The group's dislike of Jennifer didn't initially start that way, but over time, Angela began to get paranoid that her boyfriend, Ricky, was having an affair with Jennifer. She thought she'd overheard Ricky telling Jennifer he loved her, and instead of confronting her boyfriend or asking her friend what was going on, she took a much more macabre route to handle the situation. She devised a plan to invite Jennifer over with the sole intention of humiliating her violently.

The group had also lied to her about the location of the sleepover. When Jennifer arrived, she was unknowingly walking into Ricky Smyrnes' apartment. Expecting to be greeted with a warm welcome, the atmosphere turned as cold as ice as soon as the vulnerable 30-year-old walked into her "friends" apartment. Angela accused Jennifer of being pregnant with Ricky's baby. It's unclear where she got this idea from since Jennifer certainly wasn't with child, but it could have been that Angela made it up to help evoke feelings of outrage from the other members of the group. After all, she needed their help in utterly humiliating Jennifer, and the more disgust they felt toward her, the more likely they'd participate in an orchestrated attack.

Jennifer was shocked about the accusations thrown her way, as well as the hostility she was getting from her former friends. No matter how much she pleaded her innocence, the group was cruelly taunting her and getting more and more aggressive in their acts. They stripped her of her purse and took the little amount of money she had, her cards, and her phone. Once they'd finished pillaging her purse, they poured a drink into it, rendering it unusable. This was just the beginning of 36 hours of torture and humiliation for Jennifer.

Angela, Melvin, Ricky, and Amber took it in turns to beat their captive. They took a pair of scissors and clipped away at her mid-length hair, leaving nothing but random tufts sticking up. At Angela's insistence, the group set about kicking Jennifer in the stomach to rid her of the "baby" she was supposedly carrying. They took a bottle of nail polish and began drawing on Jennifer's face.

Jennifer's pleas and cries did nothing to stop the depraved group from escalating their obscene - and senseless - attack on the young woman. They stripped her naked and pinned her down before rubbing spices in her eyes. Jennifer's screams echoed to neighboring houses, who'd also heard loud banging coming from Ricky Smyrnes' property. Frustratingly, none of the neighbors contacted the police about these disturbing noises. This gave the grotesque group even more leeway to torment Jennifer further, which they certainly did. Jennifer was forced to drink an entire bottle of cooking oil. She was wrapped in Christmas tree lights and forced to stand and pretend to be a tree.

After hours of enduring this sickening violence, she was flung into a wardrobe and had the door shut tightly behind her. While a bloodied and beaten Jennifer was sobbing in the closet, the group of six sat and contemplated what they'd do with their victim.

It wasn't long before Melvin Knight dragged Jennifer from the wardrobe and to a secluded room. Here, he raped her. After his sickening assault, the brute brought Jennifer to the living room, where the group resumed their attack. The victim was hit with bottles, had oatmeal thrown on her, and was treated with utter contempt. The four main attackers - Angela, Ricky, Melvin, and Amber - left the house of horror at some point, leaving Jennifer with Robert and Peggy.

Robert and Peggy, while participating in the hostage-taking of Jennifer, didn't actively take part in her torture. Still, they sat back and watched the whole vile attack unfold without any sign of their consciences telling them to get the injured young woman medical attention. Jennifer tried pleading with their human side, begging Robert and Peggy to set her free. The pair refused.

Realizing that this might be her one and only opportunity to escape, Jennifer made a bolt for the front door. Robert and Peggy raced after her and stopped her dead. As soon as the rest of the group returned, the duo told them how Jennifer had dared to try to escape. As you can imagine, this unleashed even more violent abuse, this time dealt with sickening force.

Bleach was poured down her throat, and she was forced to drink urine. The group poured nail polish into Jennifer's mouth and made her eat human waste. The things Jennifer was forced to endure are beyond most people's comprehension - we simply couldn't imagine these things taking place. Even when we think about how we could treat our worst enemy or someone deserving of karma, we don't imagine the depravity that Jennifer experienced. The sick individuals who participated in her torture for 36 hours didn't once stop to comprehend what they were doing was despicable. If they did, they carried on anyway.

Angela and Amber each took a weapon - one of them had a crutch, the other a metal towel rail - and took turns raining blows onto Jennifer. Her body, her limbs, and her face must have been searing with pain, but she refused to relent to her numerous injuries.

Jennifer was yet again thrown into the closet while her attackers held a meeting to decide their victim's fate. Every single member of the group voted for Jennifer to be killed. They forced her to write a suicide note that explained she'd not been happy for a while and that she felt that everybody would be better off without her.

The group crumpled the note up and stuffed it in Jennifer's back pocket. Ricky got a knife and handed it to Melvin, who asked Jennifer if she was ready to die before piercing her lung with the blade. Still, Jennifer clung to life. Even at this point in her ordeal, if help had been sought, she could have survived. This possibility was seemingly crushed when Ricky grabbed the knife and stabbed her yet again, multiple times. The group left Jennifer in the bathtub to bleed out and die.

Except she didn't.

The gang returned later to check that their victim had died, and to their surprise, she was still breathing - just. Yet again, if help had been sought at this point, despite the prolonged and brutal torture she'd endured, Jennifer could still be here today. If this scenario had turned out differently, Jennifer would be in her 40s now, would have got that job as a mechanic she so longed for, would have finally got her own home and could have had the family she dreamed of.

Instead, Ricky and Melvin cut Jennifer's wrists and wrapped Christmas lights around her neck and pulled tightly. There was no chance of surviving this final, brutal attack. She was dumped in a trash can near the local school.

It wouldn't be long before Jennifer's body was discovered, though. A truck driver noticed the oddly placed trash can and looked inside. What he found will probably haunt him for the rest of his life: the mangled, abused body of a young woman. Police were immediately called, and, heartbreakingly, Jennifer's mother was called upon to formally identify her daughter. The six culprits were soon arrested. To add insult to injury, Melvin and Amber had changed Jennifer's voicemail message to say, "You're through to Melvin and Amber."

Once in police custody, the group turned on one another. In particular, Melvin Knight told the authorities, in great detail, about the torture Jennifer had endured. All six members of the gang, dubbed "The Greensburg Six" by the press, were charged with murder.

The trial began in November 2010. Prosecutors, fuelled by the sheer wickedness of the crime, sought the death penalty for all members of the group apart from Angela, who was underage and therefore ineligible. In an unsurprising turn, Amber and Robert agreed to testify against the other members in exchange for a plea bargain. This took the possibility of a death sentence off the table for them.

In court, the shocking tale was retold, and Angela was described as the orchestrator, while Ricky was named as the most eager of all the attackers when it came to violently beating Jennifer.

Various testimonies also painted the group out to be dangerous individuals.

Angela's neighbor told how he'd spoken to her days prior to the killing, where she confessed she was going to "kill that bitch" when talking about Jennifer. While awaiting trial, Angela's cellmate would testify that the teen was giddy at the sight of herself on local TV news, jumping up and down on her bed as the grim story was told to viewers.

The group, while all found guilty of Jennifer's murder, had varying sentences depending on their role in her death. Peggy Miller got 35 to 74 years behind bars. At her trial, she expressed regret over her inaction to save Jennifer but refused to face the Daugherty family. Robert Masters got 30 to 70 years with the aid of a plea deal. Amber Meidinger also narrowly missed out on the death penalty by testifying against her former friends.

The more active members in the killing - Ricky Smyrnes and Melvin Knight - were handed the death penalty. Both of the killers appealed their sentences, unsuccessfully. They will die by lethal injection, by far a more peaceful death than they granted Jennifer, whether you agree with the death penalty or not.

Angela Marinucci got life in jail without the possibility of parole. However, this was reviewed in 2022, and her sentence was changed. She will now be eligible for parole in 2070.

Jennifer's sister, Joy, would later say how she wished she could go back in time and treat her sister differently, not insist on Jennifer acting like an adult or being so independent. While she was a grown woman, her mind would always remain childlike, and the independence Jennifer so greatly desired would allow predators like the Greensburg Six to take advantage of her vulnerability. Talking about the killers' sentences, Jennifer's step dad would say they offered no closure to the family.

Three's A Crowd

It's not uncommon for teenagers to fall out with one another or have petty arguments. Often, it's about something trivial, like relationships or who's best friends with whom. It may not seem trivial to the teens at the time, but they tend to get over themselves and either patch things up or move on from the friendship. However, the tragic tale I'm about to cover begins with a teenage falling out - but it ends in murder.

Growing up in sun-drenched 1970s Southern California, Michele Avila and Karen Severson had been inseparable since they were eight years old. The girls would spend a great deal of their time together, both in school and at their respective homes in the San Fernando Valley. As they grew up, their laughter-filled chats became less about dolls and toys and more about boys and relationships. Michele had grown to be considered beautiful by both her male and female peers. She had striking green eyes and flowing black hair and was popular with the other students at San Fernando High School. In particular, boys began paying extra attention to Michele, who was affectionately known as "Missy" to those closest to her. While on the outside, it seemed like everyone adored Michele. It also appeared that her rising popularity brought out the green-eyed monster in those closest to her, as is sadly often the case.

Along with Karen, Michele was also friends with fellow teen Laura Doyle, and the trio were incredibly close - or so it seemed. They'd confide in each other about the boys they were dating and ask each other for advice or their opinion of their relationship. While plenty of teenage girls can maintain a three-way friendship, oftentimes, there ends up being one who gets ostracized or left out. In this case, it was

Michele who was covertly pushed out of the group. Her two friends ended up turning on her because they felt Michele was neglecting them to spend more time with boys.

Around this time, Karen fell pregnant and dropped out of high school temporarily. The divide between the girls grew bigger during this period, with Michele being made fun of by Karen and Laura behind her back. Karen also spread rumors about Michele, telling the other girls they associated with that Michele was sleeping with their boyfriends. The lies about Michele's "promiscuity" and secret sexual partners got the innocent teen into trouble; she was beaten up for her supposed indiscretions with other people's boyfriends.

It seems that Michele never worked out that it was her friend who was spreading these rumors about her. After all, Karen had always been Michele's protector. Out of the two of them, Karen was the tougher one, the one who would stand up to their bullies and use her sharp tongue to ward off any peers who dared torment them. Despite drifting apart, Michele couldn't imagine her once fierce defender spewing such hate-filled lies about her.

After Karen had given birth, she returned to high school, but the friendship group just wasn't the same. While Karen and Laura put on a friendly face when Michele was around, they would talk of her with disdain behind her back. The trio had disbanded into a duo.

While they were in junior year in high school, Michele began dating Randy, who was renowned for being the life of the party. However, Randy's love of socializing and drinking soon grew weary for Michele, who was quickly sick with Randy's wild lifestyle. She ended the relationship, and he promptly moved on with Karen. The young couple got an apartment together shortly after becoming an item. Michele didn't seem too fazed by her ex and her ex-best friend getting together and would attend parties where the two would show up. She made it clear she didn't want to be with Randy and that she felt no ill will against her friend for hooking up with him.

Despite this, Karen felt threatened by Michele. She spotted her boyfriend getting overly close with Michele at a party, apparently catching Randy pawing at Michele and trying to pull her onto his lap flirtatiously. This maddened Karen, whose anger was aimed at Michele rather than Randy. She was convinced her longtime friend was looking to rekindle the relationship with Randy and confronted her in the local park days later. Other girls who were at the park that day say Karen tore into Michele verbally before threatening her with a broken beer bottle. They also spoke of how Karen began physically assaulting Michele, pushing her between verbal taunts and slapping her face. Less than two weeks after this nasty confrontation, Michele would be dead.

After the incident in the park, a cruel rumor circulated about Michele sleeping with Randy behind Michele's back. Things were tough for the teen during this time. Not only had her friends turned their back on her, but they were also treating her wickedly. Her once best friend had assaulted her, her peers were talking about her behind her back, and she had no way to disprove or stop the gossip being spread about her. The 17-year-old felt vulnerable, although she had no way of knowing the true extent of the malicious words being spoken about her. Karen and Laura had thought of a plan to teach Michele a lesson she'd never forget, and on October 1, 1985, they set about acting it out.

While Karen wasn't on favorable terms with Michele, Laura had less friction with her. Laura had arranged to meet with Michele and picked her up that fateful October afternoon to take a drive. How could Michele know the danger she was in? She'd been close to Laura for years, and the pair hadn't had any direct disagreements. However, Michele had misjudged just how badly the rumors about her had spread - Laura's boyfriend was one of the boys Michele had supposedly slept with. Unbeknown to Michele, Laura was enraged by this gossip, believing it to be true.

Michele told her mother she was off to the park with Laura, so when Laura rang Irene Avila just hours after picking her daughter up, she was confused. *Isn't Michele with you*, Irene asked. She was, Laura explained, but she dropped Michele off with a group of boys while she went to get some gas. When she returned, her friend had taken off with the gang of boys, so she was calling to see if she made it home. The twisted thing is, Laura knew Michele wasn't home - she knew she'd never make it home again since she was lying face down in a stream in Big Tujunga Creek.

That October afternoon, Laura had taken Michele to an unfrequented area in Angeles National Forest, where she and Karen accosted their former friend.

Deep in the forest, they yelled at Michele, shouting at her for stealing their boyfriends and ruining so many relationships. Circling her, they listed off the rumors about her, believing them to be true, before the pair set about attacking a terrified Michele. They punched her hard in the face, they pushed her toward one another and grabbed fistfuls of her hair to pull her about. The attack saw the girls drag their victim to a nearby stream and push her face first into the water. Despite the shallowness, the girls managed to submerge Michele's face into the water long enough to drown her. As she lay lifeless in mere inches of water, the girls added insult to injury by locating a heavy log nearby and carrying it to Michele's body. They cruelly dropped it on her, ensuring she couldn't make her way out of the shallow grave they left her in.

The pair then made the 45-minute drive home before Laura called the Avila residence to feign concern for Michele. Irene was apprehensive about her daughter's whereabouts but imagined nothing bad had happened to Michele. However, days passed, and her daughter didn't come home. While Michele was your typical teen, not always the best at adhering to curfew, she'd never stay out for days without getting in touch. She knew her family would be worried. Plus, her mother did not know who she'd be with. Four days after Michele had left the Avila home for the last time, Irene received the news she'd been dreading: Michele had been found dead. Hikers had stumbled upon her lifeless body as they made their way through the creek.

Distraught Irene had no reason to suspect either Karen or Laura, despite them being the last ones to see Michele. After all, the girls were as distraught as she was. Laura even sent the Avilas a donation of $20 in a sympathy card. Karen was visibly affected by the murder of her friend, too. She and Laura cried at the funeral. Karen was frequently at Michele's grave afterward. Irene later claimed that Karen moved in with her to help her cope with the loss of her daughter, although Karen says this is untrue.

Whether this is true or not, there's no doubt that Karen's behavior after the discovery of Michele's body was borderline obsessive. She would cut out and keep news stories about the case, had pictures of Michele on her bedroom walls, and was known to head to the murder spot frequently. She kept a close eye on any police updates about the case. At the time, this was chalked up to grief. After all, the girls had been almost inseparable since they were eight. Karen was seemingly struggling to deal with her best friend being stripped away in a horribly cruel fashion.

On July 26, 1988, however, the truth would come out. Karen and Laura's friend, Eva, had joined them that fateful October day. She saw the whole wicked murder unfold. She took no part in the killing, but she bore the guilt of it for over three years. After trying to forget about the disturbing event she was witness to, Eva decided she had to come clean and told the police everything she knew. They quickly brought

Laura and Karen in for questioning, and just as quickly, they admitted their guilt. For Karen, she would later say this was the best day of her life. The burden of what she'd done had been eating away at her - although not enough to hand herself in. The pair - by now in their early 20s - were charged with first-degree murder.

However, in March 1990, they were found guilty of second-degree murder. The drop in the charges against them was because prosecutors couldn't be sure the murder was planned. Karen denied planning Michele's death, instead saying she just wanted to "torment" her former friend. The duo were given a minimum of 15 years behind bars. Karen's parents took custody of her young child.

The pair served just over two decades in jail. Karen was the first to be released in 2011. Laura was released the following year after spending 22 years in prison. Laura has lived a life of relative anonymity since, and little is known about her life since her release. Karen took a different approach after her stint in jail. She wrote a book about the crime and was in talks to have a movie made about what really happened to Michele, but Avila's family took her to court to stop this from taking place. As such, "Missy's Law" was born. It means criminals have to contact their victim's families before publishing works based on the crime committed.

Killer kids is a thought-provoking area of true crime. We never associate that level of hatred or violence with children, yet there are numerous documented cases of children who desire to murder another human. More than this, some of these youngsters go on to actually kill. If Karen Severson and Laura Doyle had never met, would both have gone on to kill? If Michele and Karen had never become best friends, would Karen's jealousy of her evolved into the hatred it did?

When kids kill, there's always the nature or nurture question brought up. Personally, I believe it's a mixture of both. Without knowing a great deal about Karen or Laura's upbringing, it's hard to come to a solid conclusion as to what truly drove them to believe they had the right to kill another girl. But for two young girls to harbor such venom and violence is truly frightening.

It's a loaded question with many variables, but do you think killers are born or made?

Murdered By Her "Best Friends"

All true crime cases are heartbreaking. Often, it's because justice wasn't truly served, or the victim endured a particularly awful ordeal, or because the police failed to capture the criminal despite plentiful opportunities (think the victims of Jeffery Dahmer, where the cannibal killer was free to kill multiple times in part due to the prejudices of some Milwaukee police officers). In some cases, the crime is so distressing and upsetting to learn about because it was so utterly senseless.

Don't get me wrong, all murders are senseless, but more often than not, the killer has a motive. Whether that motive is revenge or just a lust for blood, killers tend to have a modus operandi. To refer back to Dahmer, his motive was sexual; he wanted to abuse the men he drugged and to have complete control over their unresisting bodies. Or, in the case of Pam Hupp, money is often a motivating factor in murder. Hupp killed to cash in life insurance money.

Then there are crimes of passion, where a lover's tiff turns sinister, and extramarital affairs end in bloodbaths. Astonishingly, in Uruguay, crimes of passion were tolerated until 2017. If you had a clean criminal record but killed your spouse after discovering infidelity, you were in the clear.

All of this to say, rarely is a murder completely devoid of reason, no matter how ludicrous we may find a killer's rationale for murder. The case I'm about to cover, however, was senseless, which is even harder to comprehend. The killers could muster up no reason for their vile murder of a vulnerable, disabled woman. There was no money to be made, no feud or rivalry to win, no modus operandi at all in this case. The only reason that I can conclude for the murder of Gemma Hayter is that it gave her attackers a twisted kick.

To make it worse, the victim has been described as so desperate to be accepted by her peers that had she survived the horrific violence and torture her murderers inflicted upon her, she would have forgiven them.

Gemma Hayter was born in Rugby, a market town in Warwickshire, England, in 1983. Her mother, Sue, and older sister, Nikki doted on her. While they showered Gemma with love and adoration, it soon became clear that the child wasn't developing as quickly as expected. Her mother could see a stark contrast between her two daughters: one was extremely social, was picking up on reading and writing with ease, and was generally finding her way in the world without much difficulty. The other struggled immensely. Gemma would be described by Sue as "completely different from any other child I'd ever met."

Despite the family seeking help from doctors and the school Gemma attended, no formal diagnosis was made. While there was an agreement between the doctors and Gemma's family that she picked things up a lot slower than her peers, they couldn't diagnose her with a disability. She didn't quite meet all the criteria to be diagnosed with one thing or another, much to her family's dismay. It wasn't until Gemma was 14 that she was taken out of mainstream education and finally placed in a school for those with learning difficulties and disabilities. It seemed like this could be the catalyst for the Hayter family to get the much-needed support they'd been asking for. They'd been seeking help for over a decade at this point, with Sue contacting social services, the hospital, and Gemma's teachers to help get her daughter formally diagnosed so she could get the right support.

However, after years of getting nowhere, Sue admitted she found seeking help was "humiliating" since she kept getting brushed off by authorities and made to feel stupid. In her own words, she admitted she ended up being called an attention seeker after continuously contacting various establishments she felt could help her and her daughter.

While the family felt a sense of relief when Gemma was finally sent to a school that was better equipped to meet her learning needs, there was still no formal diagnosis as to what made it so difficult for the girl to keep up with her peers. The lack of support for Gemma and her family lasted until Gemma was murdered in 2010. To put it in perspective, her situation was looked into over 150 times by over a dozen agencies in the last ten years of her life - sadly, none of them would go on to give her the support she needed. Although we can never know what could've been, Gemma's family believes that she would still be alive if social services had intervened.

In the years after she finished school, Gemma took it upon herself to seek assistance in day-to-day living. Getting washed, brushing her teeth, and keeping a clean and tidy environment were tasks that Gemma found especially difficult, and she pleaded with the authorities to offer aid in these aspects. She wrote a letter to the council outlining what she needed help with and things she wanted to work towards, such as having a job.

While she was never offered help with these things, she was given a council flat, which offered the young woman the independence she was longing for. She never got the help she requested to help her integrate into society where she could make like-minded friends or find work. Subsequently, this left Gemma vulnerable, particularly since the area the council had housed her was known for being rife with drugs and illegal activities. It was only a matter of time before certain members of this community began to take advantage of her.

Gemma found herself befriended by Daniel Newstead, his girlfriend, Chantelle Booth, and their friends Joe Boyer, Duncan Edwards, and Jessica Lynas. The term "befriended" is used loosely here - none of the gang treated Gemma particularly well but used her flat to stash illegal drugs. Gemma complied with her newfound friends' demands to hide whatever they needed to store in her property, likely as a way to keep them from turning on her, as well as maintain the friendship she thought she had with them.

In reality, there was nothing Gemma could do to make these people truly care about her, but that didn't stop her from trying. She even began stealing from stores, only to hand the goods over to the manipulative group. The gang would put "orders" in for the items they wanted her to steal from certain places, and Gemma would go and retrieve them.

One of Gemma's family friends spotted the 27-year-old hanging around the local shops with Daniel Newstead and Chantelle Booth just days prior to her death. When she pulled Gemma to one side to have a private chat, she was concerned by what she was hearing. Gemma confessed that she was heading to Coventry on behalf of her friends to go stealing for them. When the family friend asked why she would do that, the vulnerable woman replied, "They're my friends."

Any comprehension Gemma had that what she was doing was wrong was overridden by her allegiance to the very people who couldn't have cared less about her - unless she was doing something to benefit them, like shoplifting their toiletries or hiding their heroin in her flat.

After the trip to Coventry, Gemma headed to the pub where the whole gang would meet. Daniel, Chantelle, Duncan, Joe, and Jessica were due to enjoy a few drinks together, but the fun night they had planned was abruptly brought to an end when Gemma joked with a bouncer that one member of the group was too young to drink. Perhaps Gemma's delivery of the joke was missed by Chantelle, who proceeded to punch her in the face for her comments to the doorman. Chantelle bullied an apologetic Gemma down the road, pushing and punching her as she goaded the shocked woman.

For most people, this would have been the end of the friendship. Despite the nasty attack, Gemma still went around to Chantelle's home the next day, apparently to pick up some of her things. What ought to have been a 15-minute visit turned into the tortuous hours leading up to Gemma's death.

The whole sick gang took turns to beat Gemma. They grabbed the back of her head and smashed it into a radiator. They broke her nose and tightly wrapped masking tape around her bloodied face. They stole her phone from her and put it down the toilet so she couldn't call for help. The heartbreaking irony is that even if she had her phone, Gemma was so loyal to the cruel group that she likely wouldn't have called for help, anyway.

When the gang got tired of their barbaric violence, they began to humiliate Gemma. One of the gang finished his can of beer before urinating in the empty tin. The group then forced Gemma to drink from the can. The abuse and shaming of Gemma continued through the night, and unbelievably, when the gang decided to leave Chantelle's house, they brought Gemma with them as they trawled the streets. Trusting Gemma believed the group when they told her they were walking her home. The twisted gang had no intention of taking her back to her apartment - they were marching her to her death.

CCTV captured the group walking through the streets of Rugby with Gemma struggling to keep up. It's heartbreaking to know the level of control the gang had over her meant they didn't need to check behind them to make sure she was still there. They knew she was blindly loyal and wouldn't dare leave their side. They led her to an old railway track where she was subjected to even more vile abuse.

They found a bin bag that they pulled over Gemma's head, rendering her unable to see anything. This must have been absolutely terrifying for the vulnerable woman, who eventually managed to free herself from the plastic covering her face. As soon as she did, the group pulled another bag over her head, again taking away Gemma's ability to see the fists and kicks heading her way. She was then stabbed in the back - literally and metaphorically - by the group before she fell to the ground with the deep wound dripping blood.

Not content with their level of violence, the attackers set about stamping on Gemma with such force that they left footprints on her already battered body. To add more insult to horrific injury, her clothes were stripped from her bloody and beaten body and set alight.

The fear Gemma must have been feeling throughout her ordeal, but particularly towards the end, is unimaginable. In the cold darkness, she was left to die from her myriad of injuries. She eventually choked to death on her own blood.

The spot where Gemma lay was relatively quiet, aside from a few dog walkers or joggers passing by through the day. On August 9, hours after Gemma had passed, John Irving was out exercising through the disused railway track when he spotted something that horrified him: a pair of bare feet poking out from the grass. Upon further inspection, he discovered something more macabre: a woman lying face down in her own blood. The police were immediately called, and it didn't take them long to track down who Gemma was last with. Not only was it well known that Gemma was well acquainted with the group who killed her, but they were all caught on CCTV the night of her murder, striding ahead as Gemma tried to keep up with them. All five were swiftly arrested. All five denied any knowledge of the vile murder.

The trial began in June 2011. Still, none of the group would admit culpability, nor would they show any remorse or upset that their friend had met such a cruel end. Despite their not guilty pleas, the stack of evidence against the gang would ensure they were all found guilty. Daniel Newstead, then 20, got a minimum of 20 years in jail. Chantelle Booth, then 20, got 22 years. Joe Boyer, 18 at the time of the crime, was given 18 years.

Duncan Edwards and Jessica Lynas received manslaughter convictions, 15 and 13 years respectively.

Gemma's older sister, Nikki, said of the group, "They thought what they did was fine. 'It didn't matter. It was only Gemma.' Gemma meant absolutely nothing." The crime was also sentenced as a hate crime, citing Gemma's disabilities as a factor in their abuse of her. Once the trial had ended, there were a multitude of questions regarding Gemma's care from authorities. There was a well-documented pattern of Gemma and her family asking for help, but it never arrived. A case review of Gemma's interactions with authorities highlighted 32 chances for them to intervene and safeguard her from potential harm.

Gemma's mother, Sue, said that despite the torture the group put the vulnerable woman through, she was sure her daughter would have forgiven them if she'd survived the ordeal. "Gemma wouldn't have wished harm on anybody," Sue said. For Gemma, her group of friends misused her trust and loyalty and ended an innocent woman's life with no reason offered as to why. That's the most difficult thing to try to comprehend about this case: the lack of motive. There was zero motivation for Gemma's torture and murder other than a sick desire for power over and violence towards a vulnerable woman.

Callous Killing Cousins

Relatives who kill together are a rare occurrence in true crime. There are quite a few notorious killer couples and murderous duos, but few relatives who join forces to carry out their deadly desires. In the case I'm about to cover, I'll tell the tale of killer cousins who banded together to carry out some incredibly vile acts on their unsuspecting victims. After the pair carried out sexual assaults on their prey, they'd coldly end their lives before disposing of their bodies.

Born in Florida in 1951, little is known about David Alan Gore's childhood, but he grew up to be an overweight gun fanatic, taking a keen interest in gunsmithing as a hobby. He also grew up to be a known sexual deviant. This was first exposed when he began working at a local gas station as a teen. What ought to have been a part-time job to earn some extra dollars was turned into a place for David to create his own perverse peepshow. He sneakily made a hole from the men's bathroom directly to the women's, allowing him to spy on unsuspecting victims. This voyeuristic behavior was put to an abrupt end when his boss caught on to what David was doing, and he was swiftly fired from the gas station. This did little to quell his warped behavior, however.

His cousin, Fred Waterfield, a fellow Floridian, was a year older than David. Their closeness in age saw them form a tight bond. Or rather, their twisted lust for violence towards women helped them form a tight bond. Fred's nasty temperament and David's perversion meshed together to create a truly deadly duo. By the mid-70s, the pair had decided they wanted to hunt women down to sexually assault.

Their initial attempt was, thankfully, unsuccessful. Still, for the woman involved, it would have been terrifying. The cousins were cruising Yeehaw Junction, Florida when they spotted a woman they wanted to hunt down. The woman was driving to her destination, unaware that the two men tailing her had malicious intent towards her. Fred eventually took out his rifle and flattened the woman's tyres.

Understandably spooked, she took off on foot, a wise choice that saved her life. The devious duo had lost a catch, but it didn't put them off. They headed to Vero Beach, Miami, which was rife with crowds of teens taking advantage of the sun and sand. The cousins began stalking a young girl, but yet again, their plan was foiled when their unsuspecting victim parked up in an area filled with people. Her subconscious choice of parking spot ended up saving her life.

However, the deviant cousins were persistent. Despite their two failed attempts at procuring a victim, they wouldn't give up for long.

Again, the pair trawled Vero Beach and ended up catching their first victim. They raped her as they held a gun to her head before fleeing the scene. While the 20-year-old woman went to the police about her horrific ordeal, she ended up not following through with a court case. The embarrassment of a trial was too much for her to bear, and sexual assault cases in the 70s often brought up incredibly personal - if irrelevant - details about the victim's life. Instead of enduring the traumatic event a second time, the woman chose to drop the charges.

By the time the early 80s came, David had managed to get a job as an auxiliary sheriff's deputy. This gave him an enlarged sense of authority and a badge - things he would go on to abuse. Fred had also secured employment in Orlando, so the cousins weren't together as often as they had been years prior. Still, when they did get together, they made sure to unleash their twisted desires. It didn't take long for the pair to realize they could make use of David's police badge to help them catch their prey. Fred even turned this into a business proposition for his younger cousin. He offered David money for every attractive female he could lure in using his badge. The payments could go as high as $1000 per victim, quite a significant sum now, let alone in the early 80s. The duo would stalk the streets of Vero Beach at night, looking for their next victim.

Teenager Ying Hua Ling hopped off the school bus on February 19, 1981, only to be greeted by a police officer showing her his badge. Confused as to why she'd been summoned by the officer, she was compliant to his demands that she get in his car. Unbeknown to Ying, David wasn't a police officer at all; not a real one, anyway. Once the 17-year-old was locked inside the car, the crooked cop drove her home. Not to drop her off or because of a sudden change of conscience, but to pick up Ying's mother and hold her captive with her daughter. The victims were handcuffed together before David called his cousin to notify him of his capture. Fred was finishing up work in Orlando, but once he was done, he was heading straight to the citrus grove where his cousin and the captives were.

Fred made good on his promise to pay David for procuring the victims, giving him $400, and as a "perk" of doing the job, Fred would allow his cousin to sexually assault the victims before murdering them. The pair tied 48-year-old Hsiang Huang Ling to a tree while they raped Ying. David would also rape Hsiang, but Fred took issue with her age and rejected David's offering of their victim's mother. Fred had tied Hsiang in such a tight and restrictive fashion that she ended up choking to death on the rope. To know that the woman had to watch a pair of vile brutes sexually abuse Ying before she died is heartbreaking. Once the rapists were done, they set about dismembering the bodies of the women and coldly threw the body parts into oil drums. They then buried the drums and fled the scene. The first kill had been a thrilling experience for the pair, and they agreed they'd be doing it again - soon.

"Soon" came five months later.

David had been keeping an eye out for the next woman, or women, to target. As he paroled the streets on his night shift, supposedly to protect civilians, he was scoping out possible victims. By mid-July 1981, he spotted a woman he thought would please his cousin. Judith Daley was a 35-year-old Floridan who'd moved to California. As bad luck would have it, she was visiting her native state when rent-a-cop David Gore was lurking on the same streets she was walking. He may not have looked it, but David was clever; in a calculated way, at least. In order to trap Judith, he pinpointed her vehicle, tampered with it so it wouldn't start, and lay in wait until she returned to her car to find it had broken down. Then, he acted like the woman's savior by offering to drive her to a payphone. He flashed his auxiliary badge, put the woman at ease, and she willingly got into his car. It was at this point he produced a gun and forced Judith into handcuffs.

When Fred came to meet his cousin, he was pleased with the choice of victim. The pair then raped the terrified woman before David strangled her to death. She was again dismembered, this time by the alligators he fed her to.

Not wanting to come down from their high, the killer cousins were ready for another victim. Just a week had passed since their vile assault and murder of Judith, and David was again patrolling the streets, badge in hand, looking for a woman to kidnap. He happened to find one: a teenage girl.

He flashed his badge and ordered her into his vehicle, telling her he needed to question her about something. Luckily, the teen's dad was nearby and witnessed the interaction and intervened. He went to the police with a complaint, and David Gore was swiftly arrested. Authorities took his coveted badge from him, which was the only way he could have lured a woman into his car willingly. He needed a new plan of action, and his caution from the police did nothing to panic the killer. In fact, he continued to hunt for victims and thought of a new way to kidnap them. He'd find a woman he thought Fred would approve of - after all, the more pleased Fred was with the catch, the more he paid - and lay in wait for her in her car. When the woman got in the car, she'd never know there was a man in the backseat, huddled in a ball. Then, with his handcuffs and pistol, he'd subdue the victim. He also had a police scanner to better avoid the authorities.

However, he didn't avoid authorities. They spotted him crouched in the back seat of a woman's car, holding his swag bag of incriminating items. This was just days after his badge had been taken from him. There was no way David could lie his way out of this one, and he was convicted of armed trespassing. He was handed five years in jail, but barely served two. He refused psychiatric help but was still released in the spring of 1983.

It took two months for him to resume his predatory ways. In the time he'd spent in jail, Fred had moved back to Vero Beach, and the pair soon began plotting for another kill. David set out on May 20, 1983, to procure a woman, and he did: a sex worker who knew something was amiss with the odd-looking man who was interested in her services, and she listened to her gut feeling. She managed to flee the strange client before he had the chance to bind her in handcuffs. Frustrated, David went home to Fred empty-handed. They agreed he'd try again tomorrow.

The following day, David and Fred were driving the streets when they spotted two young girls hitchhiking. They pulled over and offered the girls a lift. The 14-year-olds were runaways and were grateful for the ride. When they hopped in the van, David pulled out his pistol and cuffed the frightened teens. Fred ordered his cousin to take the wheel as he abused the girls in the back. Angelica Lavallee and Barbara Byer endured a horrific few hours at the hands of the two brutes who they'd naively trusted to give them a lift. Both criminals raped the girls before David shot them both in the head. Again, David set about dismembering the bodies. He buried Barbara's remains near Vero Beach. Angelica's remains were callously tossed into a canal close to the beach and were never found.

Four months after his release from jail, David set about kidnapping another victim. This crime would be different. The setup was the same - he'd picked up a couple of teenage hitchhikers and tied them up. He sexually assaulted them, as he had with every victim previously. But his recklessness was going to get him in trouble. He began to feel untouchable, and that would be David Alan Gore's downfall. It would also be Fred Waterfield's downfall, too.

On July 26, police were called to David's parents' house. He'd been seen outside of the property, naked, shooting at a young girl.

Just hours prior to police rushing to the Gore household, David and Fred were driving along Vero Beach, as was the norm for the twisted pair. They'd secured their newest victims: 17-year-old Lynn Elliott and 14-year-old Regan Martin. The girls were bound in the back of the vehicle as the cousins were on their way back to David's parents. On the way, Fred spotted his sister. This unnerved him; perhaps the sight of his sister humanized the girls he was about to abuse. Or perhaps it spooked him that he was committing crimes too close to home. Whatever his reason, after seeing his sister, he backed out of abusing the latest victims. This left them with just David, who tied them up in different rooms of the Gore family home and raped them.

The nightmare seemed never-ending for the girls. As David was abusing Regan in a separate room, Lynn spotted her chance to make a break for it. She jumped to her feet and managed to free herself somewhat. She managed to race to the front door and ran as fast as her bare feet would take her. She could see freedom but stumbled on the rocky footing of the driveway, where David caught up with her. The naked killer shot her in the head in broad daylight. He then dragged her body into the trunk of his car.

A young boy riding his bike along the street had seen it all. He raced to tell the police, who arrived at the Gore residence, to find the trunk of David's car dripping with blood. Inside was Lynn Elliot, lifeless for no other reason than a twisted savage felt like he wanted to rape and kill her.

David must have known this was the end of the road for him, but he didn't come out of the house with his hands in the air when the police instructed him to do so. That would require some guts, some humility. All David had was cowardice and, in the face of adversity, a yellow belly. This meant he refused to come out of the house, and a 90-minute standoff ensued. In the end, the police raided the property, and David submissively offered himself up to be cuffed, unlike the girls he kidnapped and murdered.

Authorities quickly searched the property for more victims, and they found one: Regan Martin was laid in the attic, bound by electrical cords as her naked body was tied to the beams. She was alive.

In custody, David immediately told the police all about his accomplice, Fred Waterfield. Police set out in search of the co-conspirator. Police believed the killer since years prior, he and Fred had been accused of raping a woman together. While the 20-year-old victim may not have been entirely believed at the time, it quickly transpired to authorities that, in all likelihood, she'd been telling the truth. Fred was found and arrested, and the pair were sent to trial.

With the trial looming over him and the date getting closer, David felt like he needed to get something off his chest. He met with investigators and told them about the other girls he and Fred had abducted, raped, and killed. He took the police to the crude graves of his victims, some of whom were unable to be located. Hsiang Huang Ling, Ying Hua Ling, and Barbara Byer's remains were found. David admitted that he and his reprobate relative had killed at least five women. Most of them were young girls, just children when they met their awful end.

In March 1984, David was found guilty of the rapes and killings and was handed the death penalty. Fred had to wait another year for his sentence, which would be life behind bars for the murders of Barbara Byer and Angelica LaVallee. These were the only crimes Fred was convicted of. He maintains his innocence despite being found guilty. He is still behind bars in Florida.

David Gore, despite admitting his guilt, decided to appeal his sentence. He spent years trying to have his death penalty overturned before receiving the lethal injection in 2012. His last words saw him express remorse for his crimes. However, his words and actions in jail contradicted this statement. His letters to friends would expose how he reveled in detailing his vile crimes. He wouldn't glaze over the sordid or barbaric details - he would recount them with a sense of glee. These letters saw him admit to enjoying thoughts of murdering women and that he felt delight when abusing and tormenting his victims. He also spoke of the cutting up of corpses: while the thrill of murder was exciting, it was dissecting their lifeless bodies that really aroused him.

These letters prove that if David Alan Gore had ever been given the opportunity to walk the streets again, he was an undeniable risk to women and girls. It seems quite likely - and the investigators dealing with this case agree - that there are other victims of the killer cousins out there. They could be assault victims who got free, runaways with no family, or some poor girl in the wrong place at the wrong time.

Sadly, it seems we may never find out. Fred still refuses to acknowledge his part in the crimes he was found guilty of, and David refused to recognize any more victims than the ones he offered up to the police. After all, he only told police about them as part of a plea deal. He agreed to testify against cousin Fred and reveal more victims in exchange for the death penalty being taken off the table. It turned out they found David to be an unreliable witness, causing them to reinstate the possibility of death, which is what he eventually received.

Brave 17-year-old Lynn Elliott saved her friend's life with her bravery when she ran out of the Gore residence. Not only that, but she undoubtedly saved the lives of the victims who would have come after her. Her determination to live, though cruelly snuffed out by David Gore, brought two evil killers to justice and saved 14-year-old Regan Martin's life. Little is known about Regan today, but despite the horrors she endured at such a young age, the actions of her older friend gave her a chance at life and offered her the opportunity to bring her attackers to justice.

Lord Of The Dolls

In *Unbelievable Crimes Volume One*, I covered the case of Carl Tanzler. He had an obsession with a young woman who didn't reciprocate his feelings. When the woman was diagnosed with a fatal illness, he did his best to save her with the minimal medicinal knowledge he had, to no avail. Eventually, the sick woman passed away, and Carl couldn't accept her death. He ended up digging her grave, carrying her corpse to his home, and preserved the body using plaster of Paris, among other things.

While that case was undeniably disturbing, the similar story of Anatoly Moskvin turns this obsessive derangement up a notch - or two. Moskvin isn't a killer, but his crimes are straight out of a horror movie. He would dig up dead children's graves and turn their tiny corpses into "living dolls." Anatoly is a well-traveled, history-loving, educated man who has authored several books, including some dictionaries. This is a stark contrast to what we imagine a serial criminal to be and makes this tale all the more intriguing.

Born in September 1966, little is known about Anatoly Moskvin's childhood, apart from the small snippets of information he's offered throughout the years. Some of these tales seem too far-fetched to be true, although nobody but Anatoly knows what really happened, so we have no choice but to take them as they are. One such tale took place when Anatoly was 13 years old in his native Russia. It was a dull afternoon in 1979, and the teen was walking home from high school in Gorky, a big city filled with historic buildings and bustling with industrial noise. While making his way home, he alleged he was accosted by a group of nearby funeral goers who were mourning the loss of an 11-year-old girl. The group apparently dragged a confused Anatoly along with them as they celebrated Natasha Petrova's short life. However, it got much more bizarre for the young boy.

Anatoly was reportedly made to kiss the girl's corpse, with an adult pushing the boy's head down so he could peck the face of the child. While it may have been strange for the young boy at first, he soon began repeatedly kissing the girl. Afterward, he was then asked if he'd be Natasha's husband. Anatoly was given a ring - it's not been ascertained where a pair of wedding rings came from - and the deceased "bride" was also given one by her mother. The adults "married" the youngsters in a strange ceremony of sorts.

The peculiar events that day are said to be the catalyst for Anatoly's obsession with corpses, graveyards, and mummification. What I call peculiar here is something Anatoly would later call "useful." He felt this way because that day also exposed him to his interest in magic, something he intertwined with his fascination with young dead girls.

After this, the boy would walk through the local graveyards, soaking up the somber atmosphere and taking note of all the recently buried graves. As he grew up, Anatoly proved to be an intelligent, thoughtful young man, taking a keen interest in history, particularly Celtic folklore. This tied in with his graveyard obsession, which hadn't dampened over the years. Celtic folklore includes tales of death and questions about what happens after you die, something Anatoly connected with. Pretty soon, this led to an interest in the occult.

When he wasn't reading about his interests from his extensive collection of books, he was taking long walks around the local cemeteries. Anatoly was fascinated by burial rituals and knew the cemeteries like the back of his hand. He would write pages of notes dedicated to each cemetery he visited, going over the vast history of the graveyard as well as his observations of the burial site. These walks would be ample, seeing the keen historian walk up to 20 miles a day on his observational trips. He'd sustain himself by drinking puddle water and sleeping on bales of hay in nearby fields.

Soon, though, simply observing wouldn't be enough. He wanted to get closer to his fascination.

On one cemetery trip, Anatoly took his obsession to a new level by getting into a coffin that had been left out for a funeral the following day. He slept in the coffin, further unlocking a new aspect of his unusual interest.

All the while, Anatoly was keeping down a successful and well-respected career. He'd been a lecturer in Celtic studies at the local university, penned a number of books, was a regular contributor to the local paper, and intermittently took on journalism jobs. He was well known for his knowledge of cemeteries in the local area, and Anatoly was proud of the fact that anything he didn't know about death wasn't worth knowing.

Nizhny Novgorod Oblast was Anatoly's stomping ground, and he was said to have visited over 750 cemeteries in this area in a two-year period. That works out at just over one cemetery per day. During this time, Anatoly was questioned by police occasionally relating to graves being disturbed and stolen from. Around this time, a significant number of graves had been tampered with. It had been noted that Anatoly was never too far from the grave disturbances when they took place. However, as soon as the strange man offered police evidence of his academic achievements and assured them he was visiting graveyards for work, he was quickly told he was free to go.

As a result of the unknown grave robber, police amped up their presence at the cemeteries. An alarming number of graves had been dug up, and authorities began to think the crimes were being carried out by extremists. However, the elusive graverobber evaded capture, managing to tamper with graves and make their getaway before the police could apprehend them. That was until 2011.

A terrorist attack took place at Domodedovo airport in January of that year, killing 35 people and injuring 173. The tragic incident was carried out by a self-professed jihadist, meaning authorities were on high alert for any kind of extremism, particularly if it was motivated by race.

Around the same time, cemeteries in Nizhny Novgorod Oblas were reportedly being violated and destroyed. It seemed like it was Muslim graves, in particular, that were being targeted. Under the assumption it was a misguided attempt at retribution, police headed to the local cemeteries, where they'd find their culprit: well-known grave meddler Anatoly Moskvin.

It's hard to say whether the police would have suspected him right away since he was known to roam the area frequently, and his strange passion for graves was common knowledge. Still, he was questioned by police, but this time, their line of questioning ended with them asking to go back to Anatoly's home with him. He obliged.

Officers were invited into the Moskvin residence, where they were greeted with an awful stench. The smell wasn't familiar, but the police thought it to be something decomposing - the smell of death. As officers walked further into Anatoly's apartment, they found he had a large collection of dolls. These dolls of varying sizes were undeniably creepy; they weren't like the dolls young children would play with. They were odd-looking. Upon further inspection, you could see the dolls were dressed in nice clothing, wearing knee-high boots and pretty dresses. Unusually, the dolls' hands had been hidden, with mittens or fabric covering them. One intrigued officer reached out to one of the dolls to touch it but accidentally knocked the fragile figure over. When the doll landed on its side, it began to play a sweet melody. A music box had been inserted inside the doll.

Suspicious offices scoured the apartment, unsettled by what they were surrounded by. Not only did this grown man collect and dress up dolls, but he also had dozens of pictures on show of graveyards, he had plaques taken from gravestones hung up in his living room, and maps detailing the local cemeteries were laid out.

A closer look at the dolls on display - almost 30 of them in total - saw it dawn on officers that these might not be dolls after all. Some dolls had the plaques from their gravestones placed next to them. One doll had a tag on her that noted a date and cause of death. It became terrifyingly clear these dolls were not made of porcelain or fabric - they were, in fact, human remains. The fragile, decomposing corpses had been tampered with by Anatoly to preserve them as best he could. Where their eyes had decomposed, he placed buttons or small eyes from plastic dolls. To make sure the corpses' faces stayed intact, he pulled tights around their heads. When this didn't work, he'd use the face of a real doll and place it over the corpses. Make-up and wigs helped disguise the decomposition of the corpses, as well as nail polish and wax masks.

Anatoly says he'd sit and watch cartoons with his brood of stolen children. Some of the "dolls" fell out of favor and found themselves relegated to his garage. He says these are the dolls he shunned after growing sick of them. The ones who remained in his good graces would get to stay in the main house. He knew the girls' birthdays from their respective gravestones and would celebrate each one with a party.

The man was swiftly arrested and taken in for questioning. The community was shocked and needed to know why such a well-respected and prominent figure would carry out such disturbing acts. His parents were just as surprised and appalled by their son's behavior, although you might find this hard to believe, considering they lived with him. They knew of the dolls and his obsessive collection of graveyard paraphernalia but didn't suspect anything was awry.

In police custody, Anatoly willingly answered all questions thrown his way. He loved his "girls," he told officers, insisting his motivation behind his crimes was to get the corpses out of the cold and take care of them. Plus, he was lonely, he admitted, and he longed to have children of his own. This proved difficult since he'd never been in a relationship and had never been intimate with a woman. He had tried to adopt a child, but the adoption agency rejected Anatoly, apparently because he didn't earn enough money.

To alleviate his loneliness and desire for children, he took the next best option he could think of: steal their corpses from the graveyard and preserve them at home. He said that he thought science would evolve to bring the deceased back to life, and he hoped to take care of the corpses until that day came. The youngest body was a three-year-old girl. In order to determine which graves to take the body from, Anatoly admitted he would scan the obituaries to seek out children who'd recently died. From there, he'd sleep on the child's grave to see if their spirit would "speak" to him and tell him they wanted to return home with him. To further preserve the body, he'd stuff the corpse with rags and would store the possessions the victim had been buried with inside their body.

While a full confession wasn't hard to get from Anatoly, police also had some forensic evidence tying the man to the scenes of the crimes. His footprint was found to be a regular one near the violated graves, further adding to the proof against him.

The actual number of dolls found hasn't been verified, but it's between 26 and 29. One of the bodies had been sitting in Anatoly's apartment for almost a decade. Was he sorry for his crimes now that he'd been caught? Not one bit. "You abandoned your girls," he said to the victim's parents. "I brought them home and warmed them up."

This rationalization of his bizarre and disturbing crimes was met with understandable outrage from the dozens of parents affected, most of whom were traumatized by their children being dug up and tampered with. All bar one scolded Anatoly for his actions. They were distraught at the fact they'd been visiting their child's grave all this time, not knowing their offspring wasn't in their coffin at all.

The community was stunned. While Anatoly was known as "quirky" and for being a bit different, none of them imagined what he was doing behind closed doors. They also spoke highly of his parents, who seemingly didn't notice the smell of decomposing bodies that filled their apartment. Their neighbors were certainly aware of the foul odor coming from the Moskvin residence but didn't think too much of it.

Upon looking back at some of his journalism entries, it becomes clear that Anatoly was far from discreet about his interest in dead females. When he wrote of his graveyard escapades, he was sensual in his description of deceased women, something people put down to his "quirky" persona. In reality, Anatoly was fantasizing about mummifying young corpses and keeping them for company.

After his confession, Anatoly was charged with the desecration of graves and dead bodies as well as the vandalism of the Muslim graves. This hate crime was eventually dropped from his rap sheet as it couldn't be proven, and Anatoly was sent to a psychiatrist to evaluate whether he was liable for the crimes he committed. A diagnosis of schizophrenia saw the criminal sent to a psychiatric hospital rather than jail in the spring of 2012.

He was to stay here for an unspecified amount of time, with his progress under regular review. His treatment proved to be unsuccessful, and his stay at the hospital was renewed each year until 2018. By this point, outpatient care was suggested, although this was soon revoked, as he was found to be unfit for release.

His parents have been excluded by the community that once thought so highly of them, and since their son's crimes came to light, they have been plagued with ill physical and mental health.

Now in his 50s, it seems Anatoly is no further forward in his path of recovery. He has warned authorities that he will dig up his "dolls" as soon as he is released. As such, he's advised the local gravediggers not to put too much effort into burying the girls' bodies since he'll be back to exhume them once more. The victim's parents must shudder at the thought of Anatoly ever being released from the secure hospital that keeps him under surveillance. There's no doubt that he will return to the graveyards of Nizhny Novgorod Oblast and resume his sickening collection of young girls' bodies.

Final Thoughts

Reading true crime stories can be emotionally challenging and can leave you feeling overwhelmed, frustrated, and with an irking sense of injustice. Still, we always find ourselves coming back to digest more true crime tales despite how much it can evoke these feelings.

When I was 18, I interned at my local newspaper (and would return years later to work full-time). During my internship, I didn't expect much excitement: writing my own piece for the weekend segment and getting to know the inner workings of a newsroom were my main plans. However, on day two of my time there, I was asked to attend court with the crime reporter. As much as crime intrigued me, I was from a small town and expected to be bored out of my mind. Headline news for crime in my city was often things like "SCHOOL TRASH CANS SET ALIGHT" or "*FUNDRAISER MONEY TIN STOLEN*." Still, I didn't feel like I could say no, so off I went.

Turns out, it was a murder trial we were heading to, and the death of the woman involved was particularly brutal. When I sat in court, I was feet away from the man accused of horrifically killing his partner before dissolving her in acid. Things like this just didn't happen in my small city, and people like the man standing in front of me were only found in big cities or depicted in horror movies.

As I watched him deny the brutal attack on his girlfriend despite the mountain of evidence against him, it suddenly dawned on me that monsters don't look like they do in thriller movies or TV shows. The man in front of me was well-dressed, articulate, well-mannered, and believable. His hair was carefully slicked back, he had a clean shave, and his outfit was carefully put together. He was full of polite words like "pardon me" or "excuse me" when answering questions.

He taught me something that day: monsters can disguise themselves as decent human beings. Murderers and violent criminals blend in with society with ease, a fact so many of us can't comprehend.

After my one day in court, I followed his case almost obsessively. I didn't get to return to court for the rest of the trial, as much as I hinted I'd be happy to go. I'd grab a copy of the evening newspaper on my way home each night to keep up with the court proceedings.

By the time he was found guilty of murder, among other horrific things, I felt a close connection to the victim despite never meeting her. I knew of her family and was familiar with the area where she lived. This, coupled with the suffering she endured, really drew me into the case. When it was over, although I was glad this man got his just deserts, I was also left a bit deflated. *Was it really just deserts*, I thought. The sentence he got meant he could be out on the streets when he's 60. The woman he murdered was stripped of the chance to ever reach 30, let alone 60.

This sense of injustice remains with me through every true crime case I cover. I'm still unsure what my idea of just deserts would be, but as long as violent, sadistic criminals are kept away from people they could do harm to, that's all we can ask for. In particularly brutal cases, the phrase "an eye for an eye" crosses my mind, but then, as the saying goes, that would make the whole world blind.

No matter what you believe happens when we die, I firmly believe the violent criminals of this world will have to answer to their maker, and that's something I have to remind myself of when I feel rumblings of injustice about a case.

I'd like to thank you for picking up this book and taking the time to read it. The aim of the *Unbelievable Crimes* series is to shed light on lesser-known crime cases while reinforcing the harsh reality that such heinous acts can happen to anyone. Too often when reading about crimes - and I've been guilty of this presumption too - we think, "That'll never happen to me."

My dad always used to tell me to "expect the unexpected," and that's certainly true when it comes to true crime. As followers of true crime stories, people like you and I can often be viewed as being overly suspicious or unnecessarily cautious, but the crimes we read about subconsciously serve as cautionary tales for us.

I hope I've covered some cases that you'd not heard of and brought these crimes to a fresh audience. Once again, thank you so much for reading *Unbelievable Crimes Volume Two*. If you find the time to leave a review, that would be incredibly helpful to me and help get the book to a wider audience, and I'd be extremely grateful. To those of you who have arrived here after reading *Volume One*, your readership is something I'd like to truly thank you for, and I hope you enjoyed this second installment, too.

If so, book three includes more tales that will have you wondering just how far into the depths of depravity humans can go.

My newsletter sign-up link: *danielaairlie.carrd.co*[1]

Printed in Great Britain
by Amazon